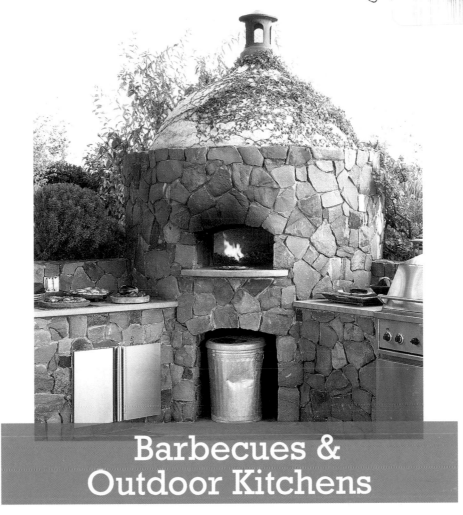

Barbecues & Outdoor Kitchens

A *Sunset* Outdoor Design & Build Guide

By Bridget Biscotti Bradley and the Editors of *Sunset*

Sunset

©2010 by Time Home Entertainment Inc.
135 West 50th Street, New York, NY 10020

ISBN-13: 978-0-376-01428-3   ISBN-10: 0-376-01428-8
Library of Congress Control Number: 2009941659

10 9 8 7 6 5 4 3 2 1
First Printing December 2010. Printed in the United States of America.

OXMOOR HOUSE
VP, PUBLISHING DIRECTOR: Jim Childs
EDITORIAL DIRECTOR: Susan Payne Dobbs
BRAND MANAGER: Fonda Hitchcock
MANAGING EDITOR: Laurie S. Herr

SUNSET PUBLISHING
PRESIDENT: Barb Newton
VP, EDITOR-IN-CHIEF: Katie Tamony
CREATIVE DIRECTOR: Mia Daminato

Outdoor Design & Build Guide: *Barbecues & Outdoor Kitchens*
CONTRIBUTORS
AUTHOR: Bridget Biscotti Bradley
MANAGING EDITOR: Bob Doyle
ART DIRECTOR: Tonya Sutfin
PHOTO EDITOR: Philippine Scali
PRODUCTION SPECIALIST: Linda M. Bouchard
ILLUSTRATOR: Ian Warpole
PROOFREADER: John Edmonds
INDEXER: Marjorie Joy
SERIES DESIGN: Susan Scandrett
TECHNICAL ADVISOR: Scott Gibson
COVER PHOTO: Photography by Mike Newling; styling by Philippine Scali. Kate Stickley, Arterra Landscape Architects; Kevin Brush, contractor; Elements Landscape

To order additional publications, call 1-800-765-6400
For more books to enrich your life, visit **oxmoorhouse.com**
Visit Sunset online at **sunset.com**
For the most comprehensive selection of Sunset books, visit **sunsetbooks.com**
For more exciting home and garden ideas, visit **myhomeideas.com**

IMPORTANT SAFETY WARNING—PLEASE READ

contents

Inspiration

There are as many design possibilities for outdoor kitchens as chefs who swear that their barbecue sauce is the best. Peruse this chapter to get ideas for your kitchen, dining area, and surrounding landscape. You may even be tempted to add a pizza or adobe oven, outdoor fireplace, or fire pit.

How to Build

Start by reviewing how 12 different outdoor kitchens were constructed. Learn from what these professional builders have done, then pick and choose elements to incorporate into your own design. The second half of the chapter covers construction techniques, including some parts of the project where you may well need the help of professional contractors. Once you understand all the ways these structures can be built, choose the approach you're most comfortable with and the one best suited to your site.

Finishing the Look

The final chapter weighs the pros and cons of a variety of finish materials that can be incorporated into an outdoor kitchen. You'll also see ideas for dining areas that are both functional and inviting, with sufficient shade and supplemental heat sources for outdoor meals throughout the year. Finally, there are helpful tips for shopping for appliances and accessories.

Inspiration

When you're looking forward to having an outdoor kitchen in your backyard, it's fun to let your imagination leap forward to the sounds of juices sputtering on the grill and the smell of dinner cooking. There are festive family meals ahead and neighborhood parties on the horizon. All the more reason to invest sufficient time exploring your design options for the project. This chapter will help you get started. It presents a variety of sizes, styles, and material choices for outdoor kitchens in several settings, from small yards to vacation homes to city rooftops. The chapter also suggests ideas for more unusual patio features, such as pizza ovens, fire pits, and open-flame barbecues, and takes a look at the comforts of the dining areas that will adjoin your outdoor kitchen.

A small outdoor kitchen just off the back porch provides enough preparation space for family cookouts.

LEFT: Prefabricated counters come in set sizes but can be faced with any finish material. A prefab unit can be a great option if you find one that particularly suits your space or you don't have the skills to build a counter from scratch as shown in Chapter 2. This example has open shelves for storage and is finished with stucco and travertine.

ABOVE: You know the feeling you get when you're outside, enjoying nature on vacation with your portable charcoal grill? Capture the same mood anytime you want with a built-in kitchen in your own backyard.

RIGHT: Reusable picnic supplies such as washable metal plates, glass jars, and cloth napkins keep waste to a minimum when you eat outdoors.

LEFT: Grill manufacturers offer large stand-alone appliances with wings for counter space and doors to conceal storage. Depending on the model you choose, however, you might spend more for a stand-alone grill than you would for the construction of your own counter. The other factor to consider is that a built-in counter can be faced with materials such as stone or brick that make it match nearby surfaces of the house or the garden so that it looks like a natural part of its surroundings.

ABOVE: Grill temperatures can be adjusted from side to side, just like on your indoor cooktop. A higher rack cooks food at lower temperatures and gives you a spot to warm up burger buns right before the patties are done.

RIGHT: What's better than a family meal outdoors? Dining facilities are not essential—just pull up a few stools from the house and you're ready to enjoy those hot dogs.

LEFT: Small outdoor kitchens can still be elegant. Richly stained wood siding surrounds this counter, which is diminutive in scale but grand in style. A raised counter near the grill puts prep work at a comfortable height, and the smooth granite countertop ensures easy cleanup.

ABOVE: When grilling is only an occasional event, consider starting small with your outdoor kitchen. Just some counter space and a little nearby storage can go a long way. Eventually, you may decide to expand for a sink or extra burners, or you may even get interested in a pizza oven. Another consideration in designing outdoor kitchens is to keep them in proportion to their surroundings. On a small courtyard or deck, a massive grilling structure may look out of place.

SUNSET ASSOCIATE GARDEN EDITOR JULIE CHAI ON
easy additions

>> Make a small outdoor kitchen more usable by adding low-voltage or solar-powered lighting in the surrounding garden. Also, a covered basket stowed under the counter can hold plates and utensils. Use the basket to cart them to the house for cleaning.

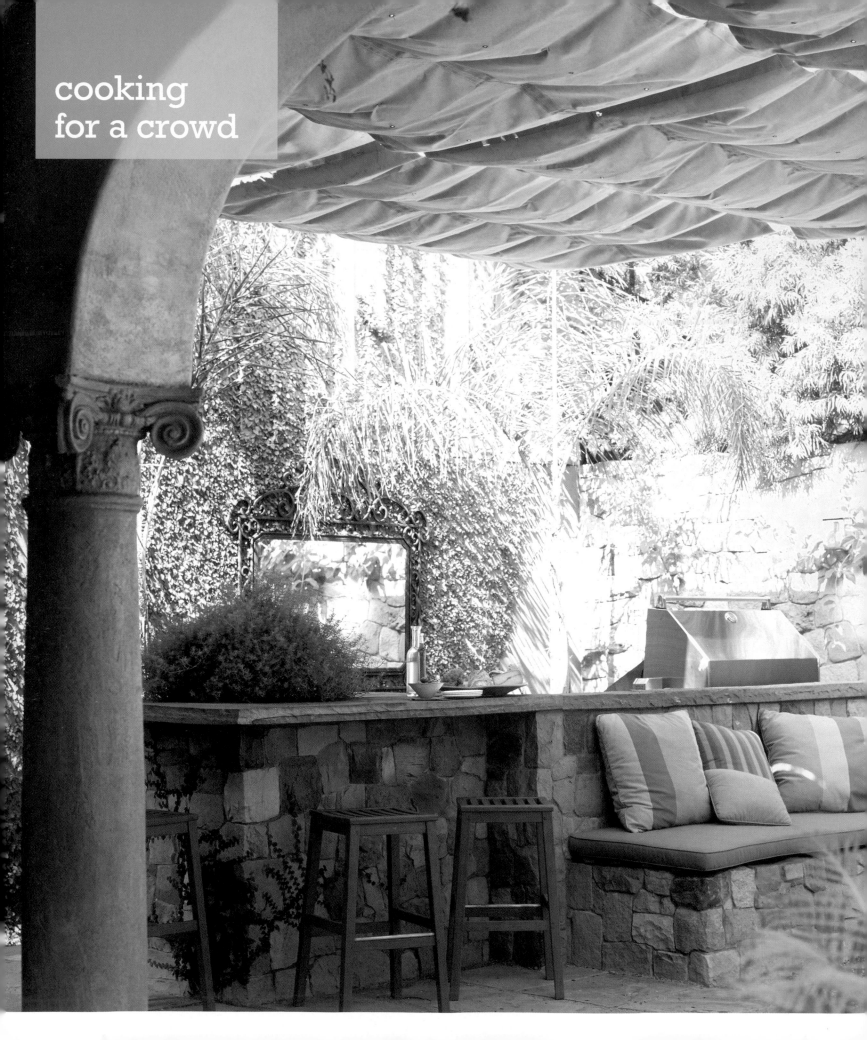

cooking
for a crowd

LEFT: Large families and those who entertain frequently will get a lot of use from a fully equipped outdoor kitchen. When you take on a large-scale project, consider hiring a designer who can help make sure you are pleased with the results. Professional kitchen designers can also suggest ideas on ways to integrate the structure into the surrounding landscape, such as adding a climbing vine along a wall. Billowy retractable fabric shades this area during midday parties.

TOP RIGHT: There's room for three at the eat-in counter, and the low stone wall topped with outdoor cushions and pillows provides extra seating when needed. A mirror placed at the back of the kitchen allows parents to keep an eye on kids while cooking.

BOTTOM RIGHT: For large patios, a landscape architect or a garden designer can help you come up with a design that complements the style of your house. Large trellises visually contain this outdoor kitchen on one side of the patio. The low stone wall curves around a table and chairs to create a feeling of intimacy while showcasing the view of the vineyard below.

LEFT: Get creative with your structures. This pizza oven could have been half the size, but the designer chose to give it a dramatic rounded top to mimic the round bunches of lavender on the hillside behind the kitchen.

TOP RIGHT: In hot or rainy climates, the last thing you want is a full outdoor kitchen that can be used only on occasion. A solid overhead will allow you to cook and eat outside comfortably in almost any weather. Recessed lights paired with oversized candle-lit lanterns make this space usable after the sun goes down. A large grill, sink, and refrigerator mean you don't often have to run back to the house.

BOTTOM RIGHT: If you plan to do a lot of entertaining, make sure you have flexible seating arrangements. This large table is on wheels and can be moved to the side when a second table is needed or when the patio will be used for other activities. On the brick pillar a pizza oven is covered with a stainless-steel plate that can be raised out of the way when it's time to cook.

15

SUNSET FOOD EDITOR
MARGO TRUE ON
cooking outdoors

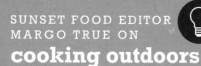

>> You can find an outdoor appliance for just about every type of cooking, so think about what you like to make most, and then decide whether you need extras like a wok or a rotisserie. Be sure to build in enough counter space to allow room for two or more people to cook together—that's part of the fun.

ABOVE: At first glance this appears to be an indoor kitchen, as many of the same design elements are used, including an upper cabinet in the corner. An open patio roof shades the area, and a ceiling fan keeps smoke from the grill from gathering. A sisal rug and woven grass loveseats mimic the style and function of a living room.

RIGHT: In a large backyard with a swimming pool, this outdoor kitchen is treated like a separate room with its own stone patio and solid roof. Curtains diffuse direct sun to make dining more pleasant. A full-sized grill, side burners, and rotisserie make it possible to prepare large amounts of food, but the owners opted against a sink or refrigerator because the grill area is close to the house.

LEFT: Efficient space planning made it possible to squeeze a full kitchen, 8-foot dining table, fireplace, and seating area onto a rooftop in the city. Stainless-steel cabinets are a low-maintenance option, and the kitchen can be completely hidden and protected from the weather with heavy drapes. A gas grill and fireplace fueled by the main gas line from the building don't contribute to air pollution as much as a charcoal grill or a wood-burning fireplace might.

ABOVE: Hidden behind tall shrubs and raised planters is a serene oasis in the middle of a bustling area. The waterfall that drops down into the table is both beautiful and practical, as it masks the surrounding noise. A simple open-flame barbecue in a small counter is sufficient to cook up the main course at dinner.

LEFT: Vacation homes are prime candidates for outdoor kitchens because you know you'll have the leisure time to enjoy them. At this beachside location, high walls with openings slow down gusty winds around the kitchen but open up on the other side to take advantage of the view. A sink allows you to do food prep and wash dishes outside while chatting with family and friends. A low fire pit fends off the chill when the fog rolls in.

ABOVE: Take cues from the style of your home and landscape when designing the outdoor kitchen. Set against a stucco house in the desert, a matching counter is topped with earth-colored ceramic tiles. It can sometimes be easier to build an outdoor kitchen against a wall of the house as gas, water, and electrical lines are close by. This kitchen has all the bells and whistles, including a sink, side burners, storage, grill lights, and a warming drawer.

design lesson

» When shopping for decorative accessories, run with the theme of your vacation spot. Cowboy hats and checkered tablecloths are perfect accompaniments to barbecued ribs in the country, while crisp linen placemats and recycled-sea-glass platters give grilled salmon a flourish at the beach.

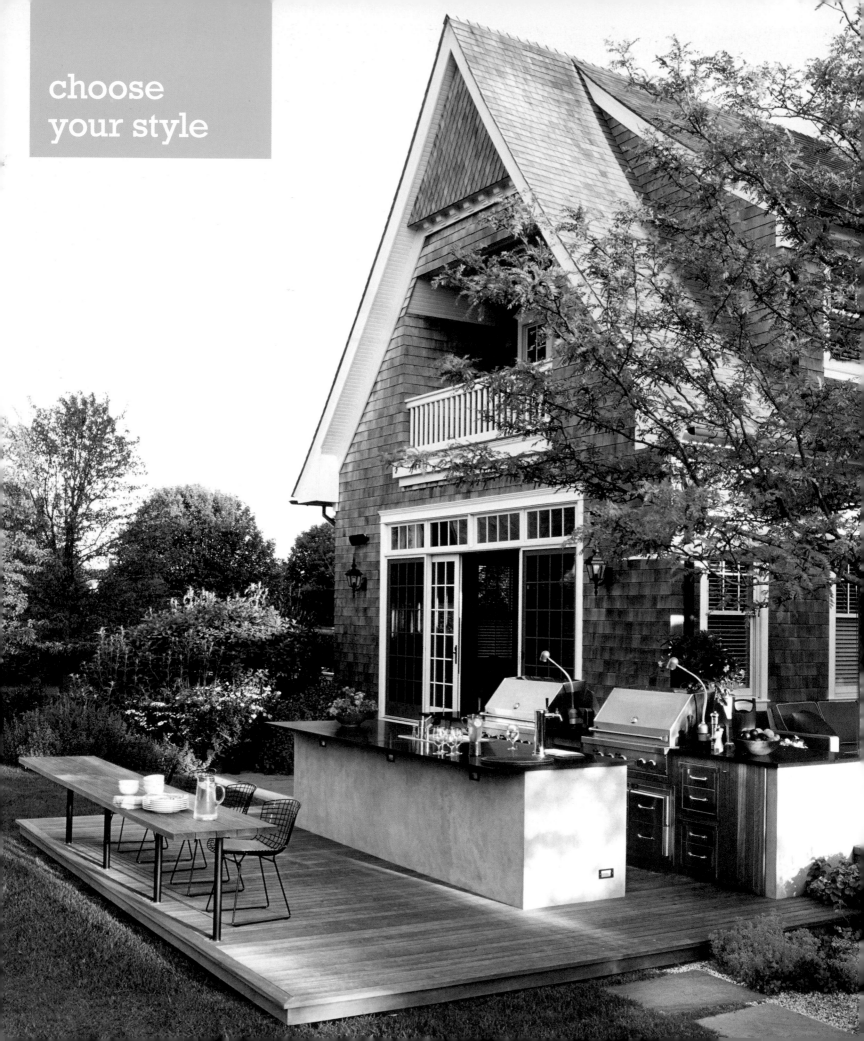

LEFT: This wood-shingled house with adjoining deck has a Cape Cod flavor. The counters are finished with white stucco on the backs and sides, and vertical wood siding on the front. Integral lights on the counters create a dramatic effect at night while flexible task lights illuminate each grill. Set up like a galley kitchen, one counter has a generous overhang so that people can pull up a bar stool and watch the action.

ABOVE: A makeshift kitchen outside a country cabin offers all the comforts of home. Instead of built-in cabinets, the owners opted for a stand-alone grill flanked by free-standing wooden buffet tables that store cooking utensils and wine. A concrete slab wasn't necessary to hold the weight of these items, but instead of placing them directly on the grass, which would likely get muddy, the owners put down rubber mats to allow air and water to flow and, ultimately, keep the surface drier.

design lesson

How will you use the space? Rustic materials such as reclaimed wood and tumbled stone will give the kitchen an instant lived-in feel, while stainless steel and a gleaming slab of granite require maintenance and care to keep them looking fresh.

ABOVE: Sunflower-colored walls and a rustic wooden table with candelabra give the feeling of a weekend in Tuscany rather than dinner in the backyard. Blue trim paint visually ties the outdoor kitchen counter to the main house.

RIGHT: Make your outdoor kitchen feel like a destination with market umbrellas and a leaning chalkboard announcing the day's offerings. Combined with the brick patio, long wooden prep tables and picnic tables to the rear are reminiscent of a summer camp by a lake.

LEFT: LED lights shine through cutouts in the wooden deck, adding to the twinkling of the city lights beyond. In addition to their sleek look, the stainless-steel cabinets are lightweight and available in powder-coat colors. Just give your dimensions to the manufacturer and they will ship you a system ready to install.

ABOVE: Part of a modern rooftop garden, the stainless-steel counter and grill are protected by a free-standing room that is open on one side. A structure like this will keep the cabinets clean and protected year-round in wet or freezing climates.

RIGHT: The cabinets complement the modern aesthetic of this landscape, but stainless steel looks great only when it's clean and protected from the elements. Applying a clear protective coat to seal door and drawer faces—or even entire cabinets—will protect them from salt, chlorine from nearby pools, and wet winters.

LEFT: Aluminum chairs are usually lightweight enough to be stored in the garage and carried to the garden when needed. Think about ways to make transporting dishes and silverware simple too, such as this square vase that spruces up the table and holds all the utensils.

TOP LEFT: When you entertain or eat outdoors regularly, a substantial dining area will feel more like an extension of the house. This large table with a concrete top and these rustic wooden chairs are heavy enough that you wouldn't want to move them around, but you won't need to with a vine-covered overhead that makes it a comfortable place to hang out in every season.

TOP RIGHT: Opt for cups and plates made of tin or plastic that are washable and reusable but sturdy enough that they won't break if dropped on the patio.

BOTTOM: Well-made wooden furniture can last a lifetime with regular maintenance. Tablecloths set the mood for various occasions and cover up any damage the outdoor furniture may sustain.

LEFT: It may take a good 30 minutes to get the oven hot enough for cooking, but it's worth every second for a genuine wood-fired pizza with a crunchy crust and seared toppings. Wood-burning pizza ovens made of clay bricks have been around since ancient Roman times. Millions of modern Italians have their own wood-burning ovens at home, just as Americans cherish their charcoal grills.

ABOVE: Cooking outdoors has been a source of pleasure since the dawn of civilization, when shiny grills and propane tanks were not an option. While there are some people who swear by their grills, for others there's nothing like a pizza oven to get the juices flowing. This example has an old-world look with a mix of brick and stone facing and a Spanish tile roof.

RIGHT: Hire a contractor to build a pizza oven from scratch using firebricks, or buy a premade kit like the one on this patio to combine with your own stand and insulating enclosure (see pages 62–65 and 84–91). Kits can include a dome, the cooking floor, a vent and chimney, an oven door, and insulation material. Depending on their size, kits range in price from $1,000 to $3,000. The example shown here was installed on top of an outdoor fireplace, which provided the necessary supportive structure and created a beautiful dual-flame effect.

open flame

TOP LEFT: A mortared stone counter houses a wood fire pit topped with a metal grate, ready for a busy grilling season.

TOP RIGHT: People in different countries have their own ways of preparing and serving barbecued meat. In a traditional Brazilian churrasco, the meat is cooked not just by the heat coming from the fire below but by heat radiating from the side-walls and top of the cooking enclosure. Kits are now available for churrasco barbecue installations.

BOTTOM: If space is tight, build an open-flame barbecue into a low stone or stucco-faced masonry wall that also functions as a seating area.

RIGHT: To cook outdoors, all you really need are a fire and a metal grate or skewers to hold the meat. This simple concrete block base lined with fire-bricks offers a flat, fireproof surface for coals, briquettes, or wood.

LEFT: These ovens are popular for baking artisan bread but can also produce a chewy pizza. To use such an oven, build a fire with wood and charcoal, then let it burn for about three hours or until most of the wood is consumed. Remove all the ashes with a scoop, clean the oven floor quickly with a wet towel on a pole, and then put your bread or pizza inside. With the door shut, the temperature in the oven should stay around 650 degrees for approximately four hours.

ABOVE: Less expensive than a pizza oven, but just as useful and fun, is a freestanding structure made of concrete block, fire-bricks, and mud or clay. *Sunset* magazine popularized this adobe oven design inspired by the classic cob earth oven. Cob is a mixture of mud or clay, sand, and straw, which was traditionally mixed with the builder's feet until it reached the proper consistency. *Sunset*'s version uses adobe clay mixed with portland cement for the outer shell. In regions with adobe clay soil, the raw materials may be available in your own backyard. If not, you can mix sand and clay to make adobe clay.

SUNSET CONTRIBUTING EDITOR PETER O. WHITELEY ON

adobe ovens

>> The *Sunset* adobe oven is a great do-it-yourself project. Check out the step-by-step building instructions at *sunset.com*. Leave the outer shell natural, paint it, or add embellishments to make it uniquely your own.

LEFT: A roaring fireplace is an ideal accompaniment to an outdoor kitchen, as it takes the chill off cool evenings and allows you to extend your outdoor time. Climbing vines make this mammoth stone hearth look as though it's been in place for a hundred years. Constructing a masonry structure of this scale requires skill and experience, however.

ABOVE: A tall brick base with a curved opening for firewood places the flames at eye level. Added on to an existing chimney, this outdoor fire place becomes the focal point of the back of the house.

construction lesson

>> While venting isn't as crucial with an outdoor fireplace as it is with the indoor variety, you do need for the smoke to draw up the chimney, and accomplishing this can be tricky. Either hire a professional to build the fireplace or purchase a kit and finish the exterior yourself. Keep plants well away from the fire and low-hanging trees away from the chimney.

TOP LEFT: A low, wide fireplace with a hearth deep enough to sit on and a mantel for displaying art mimics the design of an indoor fireplace. Make sure wood mantels and trim meet minimum clearance requirements set by the National Fire Protection Association.

BOTTOM LEFT: This outdoor fireplace kit includes a prefabricated mantel, architectural veneer stone hearth, and a tapered chimney. Many styles are available, ranging from the small and unobtrusive to the very grand.

RIGHT: It's easier to enjoy a fireplace while dining when it's built high enough on the wall to be visible from the table. When the fire is not in use, a wooden trunk topped with pillows creates an extra seating area, but these items would pose a fire hazard otherwise.

fire pits

TOP LEFT: Consider the scale of your fire pit when deciding what to put inside it. Large rocks would fill up a portable fire pit too quickly, but they look perfect in this over-sized concrete urn.

TOP RIGHT: Fire pits offer a pleasant place to warm up during outdoor parties in cooler weather. Children also love them as a place to roast marshmallows for s'mores. Lightweight metal fire pits can be moved wherever the action is. Place one at each of your seating areas to keep parties going well past sundown.

BOTTOM: A dark wall behind this clean-burning, gas-powered fire pit makes the flames all the more dramatic. Wooden benches near the fire are ideal spots to curl up with coffee after a meal.

RIGHT: Run a natural-gas line before pouring the patio for a built-in fire pit like this cast-concrete model filled with lava rocks.

How to Build

There are so many questions to be answered as you embark upon the design and construction of an outdoor kitchen. How big should it be? How do I want it to function? Do I need a refrigerator and warming drawer or just the grill? And then there's the pizza oven option! To help you with these decisions and others, we've assembled 12 standout kitchens and given you the highlights for building each one.

Of course, your site conditions and finish material choices can vary, but the descriptions should give you a solid idea of what it takes to build a similar structure. Following these project overviews, the second part of the chapter goes step by step through the building techniques needed to try your hand at constructing your own outdoor kitchen.

Nestled into the corner of a shaded patio, this outdoor kitchen is close enough to the fire pit and seating area for the cook to join in the conversation.

simplicity

Set alongside an expansive lawn, this understated outdoor kitchen has an excellent view of the home and yard. A new concrete footing was poured, but only beneath the concrete block structure of the counter. In place of a footing tied into a surrounding concrete slab, a sand-laid Connecticut bluestone patio over 6 inches of compacted base rock extends to the house on one side of the outdoor kitchen. Joints were filled with gray decomposed granite. The rest of the outdoor kitchen is surrounded by compacted gravel and redwood mulch. These organic surfaces make the outdoor kitchen feel more connected to the landscape and show that you don't have to surround a concrete footing with a concrete slab; instead, it can be nestled among softer materials.

Design

Landscape architect Keith Willig used the same fiber-cement siding that is on the house. It looks like painted wood, but fiber-cement siding is available pre-painted and requires much less maintenance than wood. A 2-inch-thick Connecticut bluestone slab with a honed finish ties in with the blue-gray colors of the stone patio, and the light color helps keep the exposed surface cool to the touch.

can I do this?

A straight-lined small counter with no plumbing is a great project for a do-it-yourselfer, especially if you hire a professional to run the gas and electrical lines. A stone fabricator should bring in the countertop.

DEGREE OF DIFFICULTY

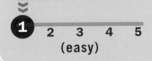

1 2 3 4 5
(easy)

WHAT YOU'LL NEED

Grill

Fiber-cement siding

Slab of Connecticut bluestone

Metal doors

Gas pipe, shutoff valve, and connections

Electrical supplies: cable or conduit with wire, boxes, GFCI receptacle

Concrete for the footing

Concrete blocks

Steel reinforcing bar

Mortar mix

Angle iron

1" x 2" pressure-treated furring strips

Circular saw

Hammer drill with masonry bit

Masonry screws

Electric drill

Galvanized siding nails

Hammer

Concrete backerboard

Pressure-treated 2 x 4 lumber

Exterior plywood

Stone sealer

BUILDING THE KITCHEN

① Excavate, Run the Lines, and Pour the Concrete

Excavate and build forms for a concrete footing that will meet local building codes with respect to such considerations as the depth of the footing and the size and spacing of the steel reinforcing bar. Hire contractors to run the gas line with a shutoff, per local codes, positioned so that the line will enter inside the counter and to lay electrical conduit into the area (see pages 100–101). This project includes one GFCI receptacle and an electrical panel on one side that powers low-voltage landscape lighting. If needed, install steel reinforcements in the footing and vertical rebar that runs up through the cells of the blocks. Pour and finish the footing.

② Build the Block Walls

After allowing the footing to cure for several days, build the block walls (see pages 106–109). Six-inch concrete blocks were used for the walls, and steel reinforcing bar extends through every other opening. Have your contractor run electrical conduit through the blocks for the receptacle on the face of the counter (see pages 136–137). Use angle iron to support the blocks that span the doorways and check to be sure that the doors and appliances will fit. Then fill the cells with concrete.

③ Apply the Furring Strips

To attach concrete backerboard siding to the concrete blocks, this builder used pressure-treated 1-by-2-inch wood furring strips. Frame the bottom and top of the concrete block counter with horizontal furring strips and then cut the vertical pieces to fit between them. Install vertical pieces at each corner and fill in so that there's a strip every 12 inches. Use a hammer drill and masonry bit to drill holes for masonry screws. Do not line screws up along the furring strips, as doing so may split the wood. Instead, stagger the screw holes. Brush or blow debris out of the holes, then drive masonry screws into the pre-drilled holes with a standard drill until the heads are countersunk into the furring strips.

④ Apply the Fiber-cement Siding

Start with the bottom piece of fiber-cement siding. Check the manufacturer's instructions regarding how close to the ground that first piece can be. Blind-nail galvanized siding nails into each furring strip at the top of each row of siding. Each layer of siding will overlap the piece below it, hiding the nail heads. Check with your local building department to see if you need a water-resistant barrier between the strips and the siding.

LEFT: Stainless-steel doors hide under-counter storage.

RIGHT: Matching siding creates a harmonious effect between the outdoor kitchen and the house.

⑤ Build the Countertop Substrate

The builder created a 3-inch internal concrete slab to support the countertop. On top of short concrete block walls inside the structure (see page 99), cut and lay pieces of ½-inch concrete backerboard so that the surface sits 3 inches below the top of the exterior concrete block walls. Use mortar or construction adhesive to adhere the backerboard to the top of the internal walls. Temporarily support any spans longer than 12 inches with plywood and vertical 2 x 4s. Add steel reinforcement and pour a slab (see pages 130–133). If your grill requires a solid support, include the concrete substrate underneath it as well (see pages 98–99); if not, you can stop short of the grill. Remove the temporary plywood and 2 x 4 supports once the slab has cured.

⑥ Install the Countertop

A piece of solid 2-inch Connecticut bluestone was professionally fabricated and installed. The overhang for the bar seating area was 9 inches and did not require any support brackets, but support may be needed for deep cantilevers, depending on the material used.

⑦ Install the Grill and Doors

Hire a contractor to run electrical lines, hook up the receptacles, and install flexible lines to the gas shutoff (see pages 134–137). Then set and install the grill and doors (see pages 142–143).

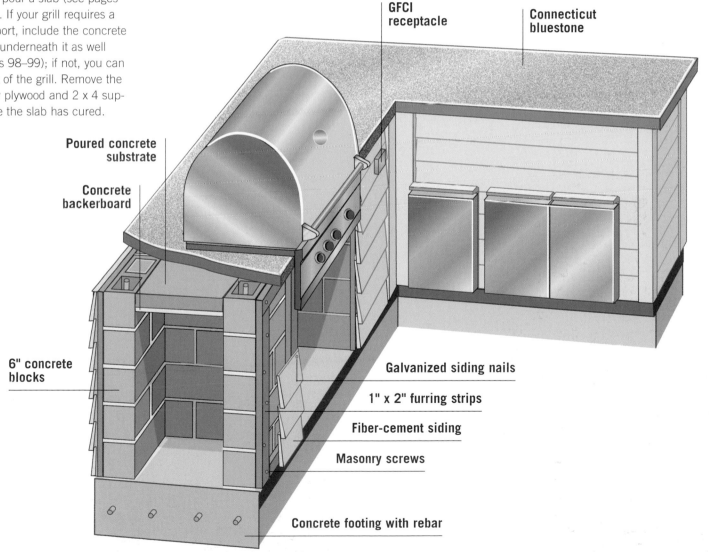

GFCI receptacle

Connecticut bluestone

Poured concrete substrate

Concrete backerboard

6" concrete blocks

Galvanized siding nails

1" x 2" furring strips

Fiber-cement siding

Masonry screws

Concrete footing with rebar

shady spot

*Karen Taylor,
Polsky Perlstein
Architects; Catlin
Landscape
Architecture;
Power Construc-
tion, general
contractor*

W ithin steps of the indoor kitchen sits a small counter that serves as a place to prepare the main course for casual outdoor meals. A sink, refrigerator, and warming drawer make entertaining convenient, but the close proximity of the indoor kitchen allowed the builders to keep the footprint of the outdoor kitchen small. There are a fire pit and built-in seating nearby for guests to linger while waiting for dinner to commence.

Design

The style of the ipe trellis and the stucco walls echo the contemporary lines of the house. The trellis provides shade during the day; at night, electric lights hardwired into the structure illuminate the counter. Carerra marble has a classic look but needs to be kept well sealed to prevent staining. It is somewhat protected in this kitchen under the trellis. Stone tiles set in a geometric pattern on the poured concrete patio surround the counter. Copper planters filled with tall shrubs that pick up on the burnt orange hue of the ipe trellis flank either side, visually softening the edges.

A simple trellis extends up from the side-yard wall and out to provide shade for the outdoor kitchen. The top of the trellis is well away from the flames of the grill. Hire a contractor to build a similar structure and make sure it is properly anchored to the wall.

WHAT YOU'LL NEED

Gas grill

Carerra marble slab

Sink with faucet and trap

Refrigerator

Warming drawer

Stainless-steel doors

Light fixtures

Gas pipe, shutoff valve, and connections

Electrical supplies: cable or conduit with wire, boxes, GFCI receptacle

Plumbing supplies: supply line, drain line, stop valve

Concrete for the footing

Concrete blocks

Steel reinforcing bar

Mortar mix

Angle iron

Stucco mix

can I do this?

Practice applying stucco on a scrap of wood before applying it to the counter if you are trying to match the texture of the surrounding wall or nearby house.

DEGREE OF DIFFICULTY

1 2 **3** 4 5
(moderate)

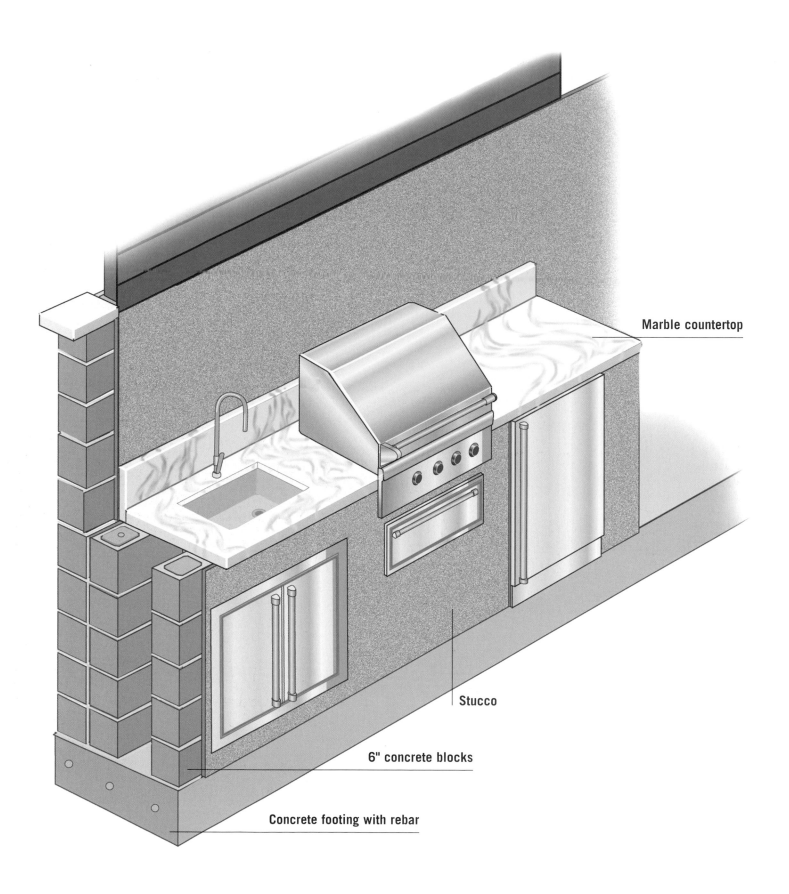

Marble countertop

Stucco

6" concrete blocks

Concrete footing with rebar

50

BUILDING THE KITCHEN

① Excavate, Run the Lines, and Pour the Concrete

Excavate and build forms for a concrete footing that will meet local building codes with respect to such considerations as the depth of the footing and the size and spacing of the steel reinforcing bar. Hire contractors to run the gas line with a shutoff, per local codes, positioned so that the line will enter inside the counter (see pages 100–101) and to run plumbing lines for the sink and electrical lines for the GFCI-rated receptacles, refrigerator, and warming drawer. If needed, install steel reinforcements in the footing and vertical rebar that will run up through the cells of the blocks. Pour and finish the footing.

② Build the Block Walls

After allowing the footing to cure for several days, build the block walls (see pages 106–109). Six-inch concrete blocks were used for the walls, and steel reinforcing bar extends through every other opening. Have your contractor run the electrical conduit through the blocks for the receptacles on the face of the counter (see pages 136–137). Use angle iron to support the blocks that span the doorways and check to be sure that the doors and appliances will fit. Then fill the cells with concrete.

③ Stucco the Counter

Apply two or three coats of stucco to each side of the counter (see pages 120–121). You can either apply a finish coat of stucco with integral color, or paint the stucco after it has fully cured.

④ Have the Stone Countertop Installed

Once the walls are built, you can have a stone fabricator produce a template for the stone countertop. You will need to have the grill and sink on site for the templating appointment so properly sized holes can be made. It might take a week or two between the fabrication appointment and installation. Because of the small size of the counter areas flanking the grill in this project, the stone has sufficient support so as not to require a substrate.

⑤ Install the Appliances and Doors

Hire a contractor to hook up the receptacles and install flexible lines from the gas shutoff (see pages 134–137). Then set and install the grill, refrigerator, and warming drawer per the manufacturers' instructions (see pages 142–143). Hook up the sink and faucet to the water supply and drainpipes that were roughed in at the start (see pages 138–141).

Bar-size sinks are ideal for minor tidying up and for rinsing produce.

small but
mighty

Keith Willig
Landscape
Architecture and
Construction;
Rosemary Wells,
Viridian Landscape
Architecture

This outdoor kitchen proves that you don't need a lot of square footage to create a functional work space. Spanning 8½ feet from end to end, the design features a 30-inch-wide by 5-foot-6-inch counter area on one side and an 18-inch-wide by 3-foot-6-inch counter on the other, allowing for a generous work and serving area. Within the counter are two sets of steel doors, a gas grill and side burner, and a warming drawer.

Design

An eclectic patio with a combination of mortared Three Rivers flagstone and ceramic tiles surrounds the counter, which was finished with stucco to match the house. The homeowners opted for the simple maintenance of ceramic tile for the counter-top, which also lets a surrounding art collection and sculptural plantings take center stage. Landscape architect Keith Willig chose to pour a 3-inch-thick concrete countertop to support the tiles rather than simply use a concrete backerboard base. "I always wonder if people will be dancing on these things," he reasoned.

can I do this?

Don't let its size fool you. Packing this many appliances into a small structure takes some planning, and a stucco finish requires practice. The concrete counter topped with tiles may take several weekends on its own, so pace yourself.

DEGREE OF DIFFICULTY
≫
1   2   **3**   4   5
(moderate)

WHAT YOU'LL NEED

Grill	Concrete blocks	Magnesium float
Side burner	Steel reinforcing bar	Hammer and nails
Warming drawer	Mortar mix	Concrete edger
Stucco mix	Angle iron	Wet saw
Tile	Hammer drill with masonry bit	Thinset mortar
Metal doors	Masonry screws	Fortified grout
Gas pipe, shutoff valve, and connections	Concrete backerboard	Square-notched trowel
Electrical supplies: cable or conduit with wire, boxes, GFCI receptacle	2 x 4s and 2 x 2s to build forms for the countertop	Grout sealer
Concrete for the footing	Concrete and reinforcing bar for the countertop	Silicone caulk

BUILDING THE KITCHEN

❶ Excavate, Run the Lines, and Pour the Concrete

Excavate and build forms for a concrete footing that will meet local building codes with respect to such considerations as the depth of the footing and the size and spacing of the steel reinforcing bar. Hire a contractor to run the gas line with a shutoff, per local codes, positioned so that the line will enter inside the counter (see pages 100–101). You will also need gas lines for the grill and side burner and electricity for the warming drawer, a GFCI-rated receptacle, and built-in lights. If needed, install steel reinforcements in the footing and vertical rebar that will run up through the cells of the blocks. Pour and finish the footing. In this project, 12-inch-long, ½-inch-diameter steel dowels were placed in the sides of the existing concrete slab to connect it to the new footing. The builder put polymer foam between the new and old concrete and covered it with mastic.

❷ Build the Block Walls

After allowing the footing to cure for several days, build the block walls (see pages 106–109). Six-inch concrete blocks were used for the walls, and steel reinforcing bar extends through every other opening. Have your contractor run the electrical conduit through the blocks for the receptacle on the face of the counter (see pages 136–139). Use angle iron to support the blocks that span the doorways and check to be sure that the doors and appliances will fit. Then fill the cells with concrete.

❸ Frame and Pour the Countertop Substrate

Cut pieces of ½-inch concrete backerboard to fit, set them in place, and make sure the grill and burner will fit in the openings. Attach backerboard to the tops of the concrete block walls with mortar or construction adhesive. Inside the counter, prop boards to support the backerboard while you pour. See pages 130–133 for instructions on pouring and finishing a concrete countertop. Construct a form for the concrete using 2 x 4s and 2 x 2s. Add reinforcing mesh that will run through the center of the countertop's thickness. Mix concrete and pour it into the form, trowel the surface smooth, and later remove the form boards and trowel the edges. Allow the concrete to cure slowly.

❹ Stucco

Apply two or three coats of stucco to each side of the counter (see pages 120–121). You can either apply a finish coat of stucco with integral color, or paint the stucco after it has fully cured.

❺ Set the Tiles

Lay countertop tiles following the instructions on pages 126–129. Lay out tiles in a dry run, make cuts as necessary, then lay one section at a time in thinset mortar. Large bullnose-edged tiles were used on the top and sides of this countertop, but you can use smaller tiles or V-cap edges as well. Wait a day or two for the mortar to harden, then apply grout and wipe the surface clean. Seal the grout once it is cured.

❻ Install the Appliances and Doors

Hire a contractor to hook up the receptacles and lighting fixtures and to install flexible lines from the gas shutoff (see pages 134–137). Then set and install the grill, warming drawer, side burner, and doors per the manufacturers' instructions (see pages 142–143).

SUNSET ASSOCIATE FOOD EDITOR
ELAINE JOHNSON ON

warming drawers

➤➤ Select a warming drawer that is approved for outdoor use. Many grill manufacturers offer coordinating designs. They are especially useful when you entertain a lot, as you can cook in batches and keep foods warm, or heat bread while you grill steaks. The temperature can be set between 100 and 200 degrees to keep food warm without overcooking it.

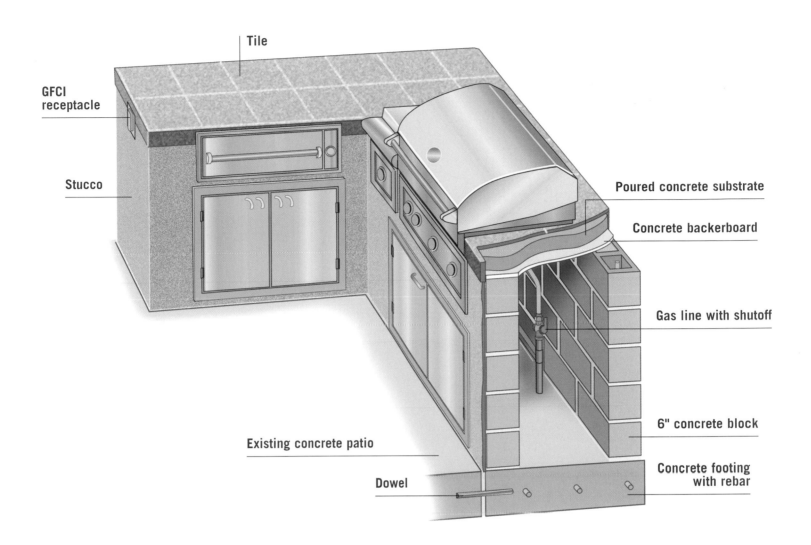

Tile

GFCI
receptacle

Stucco

Poured concrete substrate

Concrete backerboard

Gas line with shutoff

6" concrete block

Existing concrete patio

Dowel

Concrete footing
with rebar

LEFT: Low-voltage task
lights with flexible
arms allow you to see
whether your steak
is cooked properly as
the sun goes down.

RIGHT: With a warming
drawer, you can keep
batches of food warm
and serve everyone at
once when the entire
meal is prepared.

mediterranean kitchen

On a sloped lot under a large cedar arbor, landscape architect Kate Stickley designed a rustic outdoor room for year-round entertaining. In the summer, the arbor provides dappled shade, while in the winter an overhead infrared heater and fireplace keep the area warm enough for dining. Unusual for an outdoor kitchen, the cabinets contain pullouts for garbage and recycling, there's a corner cabinet with a lazy Susan to make the most of the space, and there are also storage drawers. This kind of accessible, usable storage space helps to make the outdoor kitchen nearly as functional as its indoor counterpart.

Design

A colored concrete patio for the kitchen matches a nearby pool deck to visually connect the two spaces, and the stucco color on the counters matches the house. Hard-wearing porcelain tiles in mottled tones blend with the colored concrete below, while cedar doors interspersed with metal ones reinforce the rustic design. The beautiful backsplash with grape vine motif tiles also prevents dishes from being pushed over the edge into the plantings.

can I do this?

This outdoor kitchen is packed with appliances and includes a sink. Hire a contractor to help with the hookups and focus on the stucco and on tiling the countertop and backsplash.

DEGREE OF DIFFICULTY

1 2 **3** 4 5
(moderate)

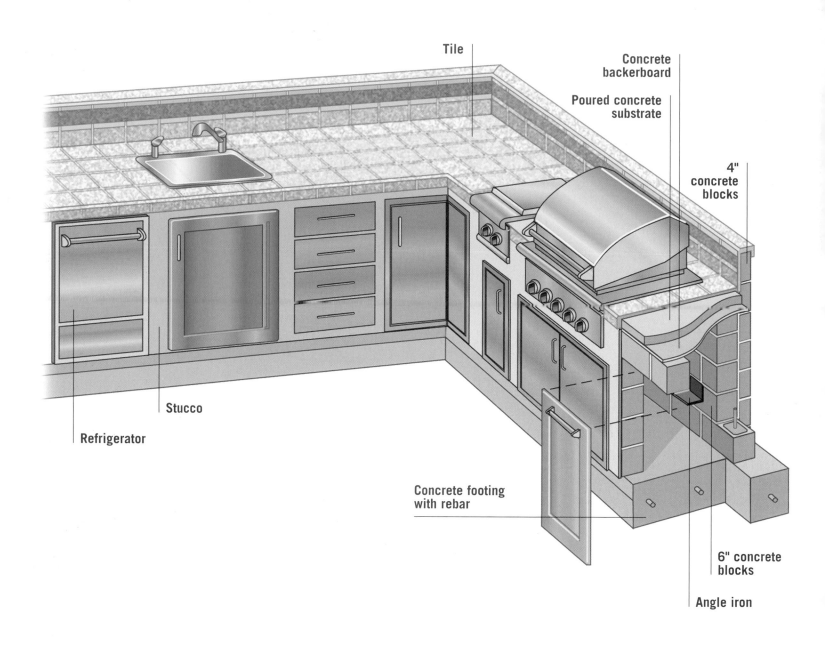

Tile

Concrete backerboard

Poured concrete substrate

4" concrete blocks

Stucco

Refrigerator

Concrete footing with rebar

6" concrete blocks

Angle iron

WHAT YOU'LL NEED

Gas grill

Side burner

Refrigerator

Sink with faucet and trap

Custom wooden doors

Porcelain tiles

Sink with faucet and trap

Gas pipe, shutoff valve, and connections

Electrical supplies: cable or conduit with wire, boxes, GFCI receptacle

Plumbing supplies: supply line, drain line, stop valve

Concrete for the footing

Concrete blocks

Steel reinforcing bar

Mortar mix

Angle iron

2 x 4s

2 x 2s

Concrete for the substrate

Hammer drill

Masonry screws

Stucco mix

Square-notched trowel

Fortified grout

Sponge

Bucket

The dining table is situated to make the most of a hillside view.

BUILDING THE KITCHEN

① Excavate, Run the Lines, and Pour the Concrete

Excavate and build forms for a concrete footing that will meet local building codes with respect to such considerations as the depth of the footing and the size and spacing of the steel reinforcing bar. Hire contractors to run the gas line with a shutoff, per local codes, positioned so that the line will enter inside the counter (see pages 100–101) and to run plumbing lines for the sink and electrical lines for the refrigerator and GFCI-rated receptacles. If needed, install steel reinforcements in the footing and vertical rebar that will run up through the cells of the blocks. Pour and finish the footing.

② Build the Block Walls

After allowing the footing to cure for several days, build the block walls (see pages 106–109). Six-inch concrete blocks were used for the walls, and steel reinforcing bar extends through every other opening. Four-inch concrete blocks were used to create the structure for the tiled backsplash. Have your contractor run electrical conduit through the blocks for the receptacles on the face of the counter and backsplash (see pages 136–137). Use angle iron to support the blocks that span the doorways and be sure that the doors and appliances will fit. Then fill the cells with concrete.

③ Frame and Pour the Countertop Substrate

See pages 130–133 for instructions on pouring a concrete countertop. Cut ½-inch concrete backerboard to fit, set it in place, and make sure the grill, burner, and sink will fit in the openings. Use mortar or construction adhesive to attach the backerboard to the top of the block walls. Inside the counter, prop boards to support the backerboard while you pour. Construct a form for the concrete using 2 x 4s and 2 x 2s. Add reinforcing mesh or a grid of rebar that will run through the center of the countertop's thickness. Mix concrete and pour it into the form, trowel the surface smooth, and later remove the form boards and trowel the edges. Allow the concrete to cure slowly.

❹ Stucco

Apply two or three coats of stucco to each side of the counter (see pages 120–121). You can either apply a finish coat of stucco with integral color, or paint the stucco after it has fully cured. If you are trying to match the texture of the house or a nearby wall, practice on a scrap of concrete backerboard until you master the technique.

❺ Set the Tiles

Lay countertop tiles following the instructions on pages 126–129. Dry-lay tiles first to establish the pattern, make cuts as necessary, then lay one section at a time in thinset mortar. Bullnose-edged tiles were used on the edges of this countertop, but you can use V-cap edges. Lay the decorative backsplash tiles once the counter tiles are set. Wait a day or two for the mortar to harden, then apply grout to all counter and backsplash areas and wipe the surface clean. Seal the grout once it has cured.

❻ Install the Appliances and Doors

Hire a contractor to hook up the receptacles and to install flexible lines from the gas shutoff (see pages 134–137). Then set and install the grill and side burner per the manufacturers' instructions (see pages 142–143). Hook up the sink and faucet to the water supply and drainpipes that were roughed in at the start (see pages 138–141).

FAR LEFT: An awkward corner becomes the perfect spot for the storage of bowls and colanders with a lazy Susan.

LEFT: A pullout trash drawer ensures trash and recycling get separated at the source.

RIGHT: Stainless-steel drawers with dividers keep small items organized.

Keith Willig
Landscape
Architecture and
Construction

Whent all you really want is pizza, there's no need to build a full outdoor kitchen with a grill. In one corner of this small backyard, a pizza oven sits just outside the doors of the house. A Connecticut bluestone patio laid over sand stretches from the house to the pizza oven and then into the yard beyond. The oven can also be used as a fireplace to make the seating area of the patio a little warmer at night.

Design

This pizza oven kit from Mugnaini arrived preassembled with the gable enclosure already constructed. The cement backerboard enclosure around the pizza oven comes weatherproofed with a layer of stucco. You can add this structure to the end of a run of outdoor counters, or create a freestanding structure like this one. Architectural stone veneer from Eldorado was selected to blend with the Connecticut bluestone patio.

Imagine creating thin-crust, wood-fired pizzas like these in your own backyard.

WHAT YOU'LL NEED

Preassembled pizza oven kit

Concrete for the footing

Steel reinforcing bar

3½" metal track framing

Self-tapping screws

½" concrete backerboard

Concrete backerboard screws

Wire mesh

Masonry screws

Stucco mix

Finishing trowel

Veneer stone

Mortar mix

Mortar bag

can I do this?

If you use a preassembled kit from the manufacturer like this one, the only work you need to do is finishing the base of the structure. There are no electrical, gas, or plumbing connections.

DEGREE OF DIFFICULTY

1   2   3   4   5
(easy)

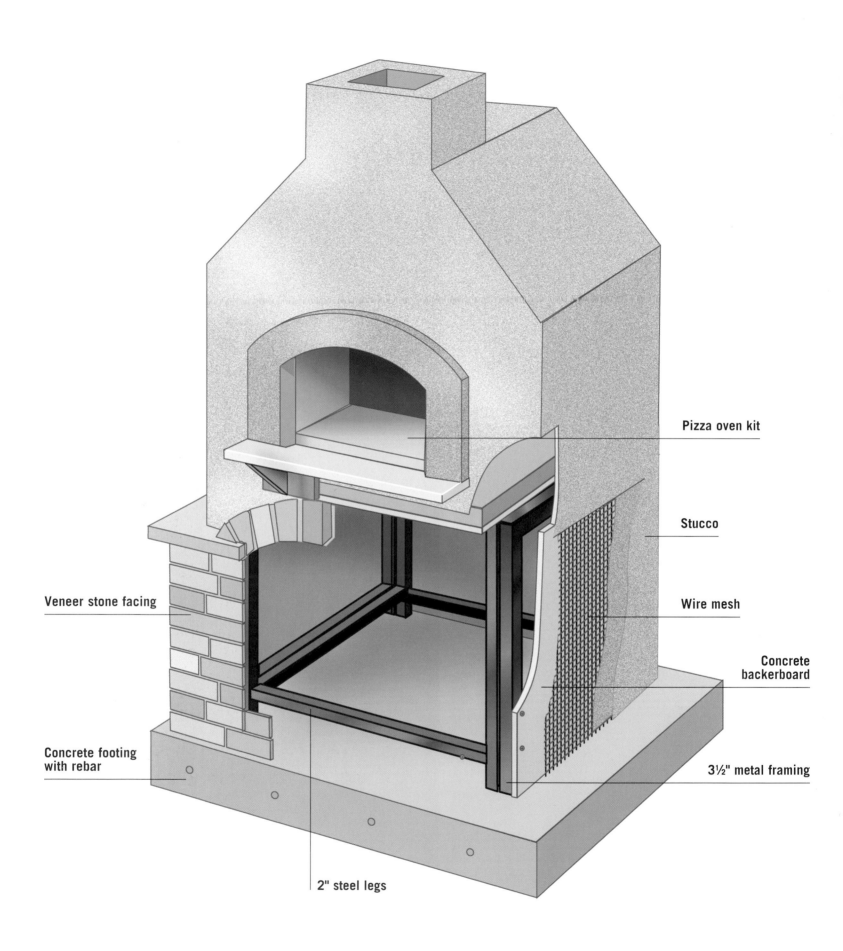

Pizza oven kit

Stucco

Wire mesh

Concrete backerboard

3½" metal framing

Veneer stone facing

Concrete footing with rebar

2" steel legs

BUILDING THE KITCHEN

① Excavate and Pour the Concrete

Excavate and build forms for a concrete footing that will meet local building codes with respect to such considerations as the depth of the footing and the size and spacing of the steel reinforcing bar. If needed, install steel reinforcements in the footing, but do not extend them up through the footing as you might if you were building a block counter. Pour and finish the footing.

② Install the Preassembled Kit

Follow the manufacturer's instructions to install the preassembled pizza oven kit onto the concrete footing. In this project, the homeowner chose the Mugnaini Medio 100 with gable enclosure. The pizza oven arrives assembled on 2-inch steel legs with self-adjusting feet. Make sure the structure is level and plumb.

③ Frame out the Base

See pages 114–115 for instructions on building with metal framing. Cut pieces of 3½-inch metal track framing to size and use self-tapping screws made for metal studs to attach the pieces, creating a freestanding frame that wraps around the steel legs that came with the kit. Then use metal screws to attach the corners of the new steel track framing to the existing legs.

④ Add the Backerboard

Cut ½-inch concrete backerboard to size following the instructions on page 115. Attach it to the metal framing by driving concrete backerboard screws every 4 inches into the studs and channels. If desired, create an opening in the front for wood storage. At this point, the concrete backerboard should be about flush with the pizza oven structure on top.

⑤ Stucco

In this project, the veneer stone was placed only on the front and partway along the sides of the structure, so new stucco needed to be added to the sides and back. Wrap wire mesh around the concrete backerboard on the sides and back of the base and use masonry screws to attach it to the backerboard so that it is taut and smooth. Apply two or three coats of stucco to the counter (see pages 120–121). The wire mesh will help the stucco adhere to the backerboard. As you work, spread stucco over the top half of the structure that came with a stucco finish. Apply additional stucco as needed until you can no longer see the separation between the top and bottom. Apply a finish coat of stucco with integral color, or paint the stucco after it has fully cured.

⑥ Apply the Veneer Stone

Follow the instructions on page 119 to set the Eldorado stone veneer. Spread mortar over the concrete backerboard, set stones in place using the manufacturer's drawings as guidance, let the mortar harden, and then use a mortar bag to fill the joints. In this project, the top was finished with a stone ledge deep enough to set drinks on.

Veneer stone with raked joints is easy to install and perfectly frames a stash of wood for use in the pizza oven.

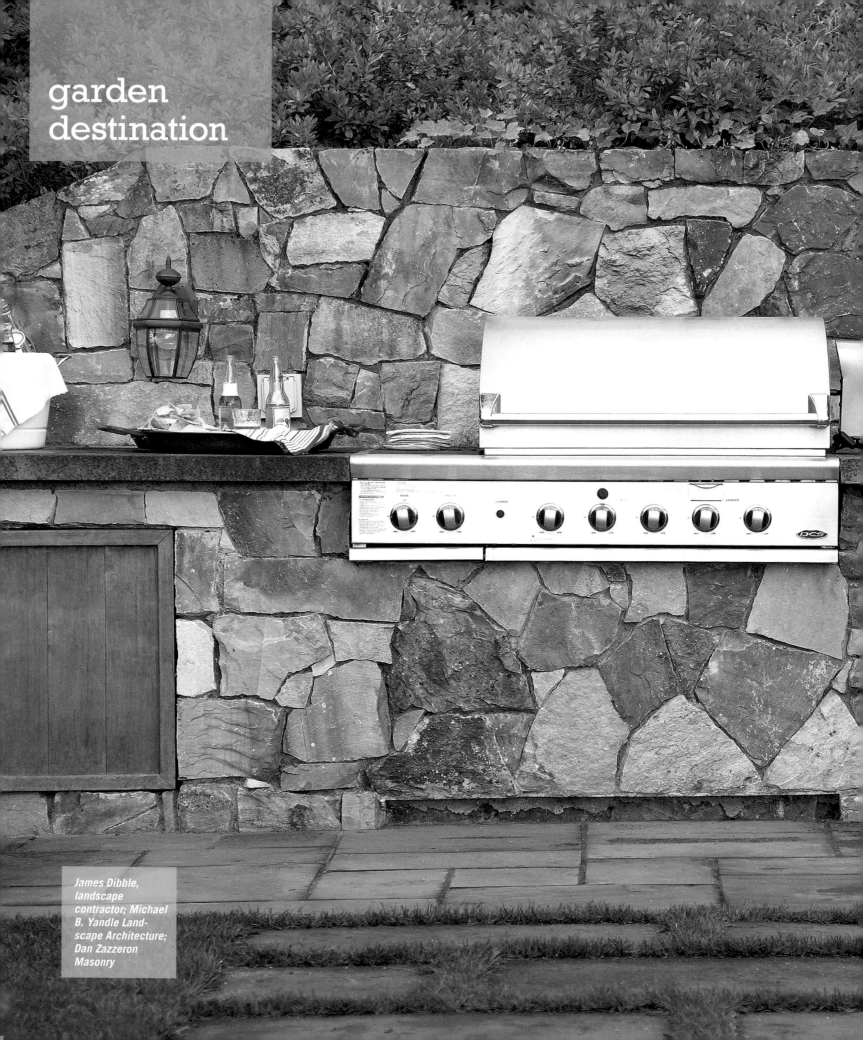

garden
destination

James Dibble, landscape contractor; Michael B. Yandle Landscape Architecture; Dan Zazzeron Masonry

Ⅰn the back corner of a lush garden sits a small outdoor kitchen built against a retaining wall and faced with randomly shaped stones that give it an English country feel. The sand-laid bluestone stepping-stones and patio are bordered by grass, and shrubs peek out from behind the ivy-topped wall so the entire kitchen is surrounded by greenery. Low-voltage carriage-style lanterns flank the gas grill and provide soft light that leads you to the kitchen at dusk.

Design

Blue Ridge veneer stone was used on the counter and retaining wall. A bluish-gray Connecticut bluestone slab on the countertop picks up the same shades in the veneer stone. Custom wooden doors keep the stainless steel to a minimum and help the counter blend into the landscape. A design feature not often seen in outdoor kitchens is the toe-kick under the grill. This allows the cook to stand a little closer while working. The builder also included an on-demand water heater below the sink so that he could use a single cold-water supply pipe but still provide hot water at the faucet when needed.

can I do this?

The counter itself is not difficult to construct without the retaining wall. Hire contractors to rough in the supply and drain lines for the sink and gas and electrical lines if you include those elements.

DEGREE OF DIFFICULTY

1 **2** 3 4 5
(moderate)

WHAT YOU'LL NEED

Gas grill

Sink with faucet and trap

Connecticut bluestone slab

Veneer stones

Custom wooden doors

Light fixtures

Gas pipe, shutoff valve, and connections

Electrical supplies: cable or conduit with wire, boxes, GFCI receptacle

Plumbing supplies: supply line, drain line, stop valve, and on-demand water heater

Concrete for the footing

Concrete blocks

Steel reinforcing bar

Mortar mix

Angle iron

Hammer

Cold chisel

Trowel

Mortar bag

BUILDING THE KITCHEN

① Excavate, Run the Lines, and Pour the Concrete

Excavate and build forms for a concrete footing that will meet local building codes with respect to such considerations as the depth of the footing and the size and spacing of the steel reinforcing bar. Hire contractors to run the gas line with a shutoff, per local codes, positioned so that the line will enter inside the counter (see pages 100–101) and to run plumbing lines for the sink and electrical lines for the GFCI-rated receptacles, low-voltage lights, and on-demand water heater (see page 139). If needed, install steel reinforcements in the footing and vertical rebar that will run up through the cells of the blocks. Pour and finish the footing.

② Build the Block Walls

After allowing the footing to cure for several days, build the block walls (see pages 106–109). Six-inch concrete blocks were used for the walls, and steel reinforcing bar extends through every other opening. Internal block walls running front to back were built on either side of the gas grill. Have your contractor run electrical conduit through the blocks for the receptacles on the face of the counter and the wall behind the counter if your project will include that feature (see pages 136–137). Use angle iron to support the blocks that span the doorways and check that the doors and appliances will fit. Then fill the cells with concrete.

③ Install the Veneer Stone

Following the instructions on pages 122–123, set the veneer stones. These stones are thicker than flagstones and much heavier than man-made veneer stones (page 119). Starting at a bottom corner, skim-coat a small area of the block wall with mortar. Set stones carefully, aiming for an irregular pattern of shapes and colors. Use outside corner stones if they are available. Shape stones as needed with a hammer and cold chisel. Back-butter each stone and rake the joints as you go.

RIGHT: Plug a low-voltage transformer into a GFCI receptacle inside the counter to power the lantern-style lights. Make sure the receptacle is accessible after construction is complete.

FAR RIGHT: The grill should be on site for the countertop templating appointment so that the front edge of the grill will be flush with the top of the countertop.

4 Have the Stone Countertop Installed

Once the walls are built, you can have a stone fabricator come out and produce a template for the stone countertop. You will need to have the grill and sink on site for the templating appointment so properly sized holes can be made. It might take a week or two between the fabrication appointment and installation. Because of the shallow depth and the interior block walls spanning the grill in this project, the stone has enough support so as not to require a substrate.

5 Install the Appliances and Doors

Hire a contractor to hook up the receptacles and install flexible lines from the gas shutoff (see pages 134–137). Then set and install the grill per the manufacturer's instructions (see pages 142–143). Hook up the sink and faucet to the water supply and drainpipes that were roughed in at the start (see pages 138–141), and hook up the on-demand water heater.

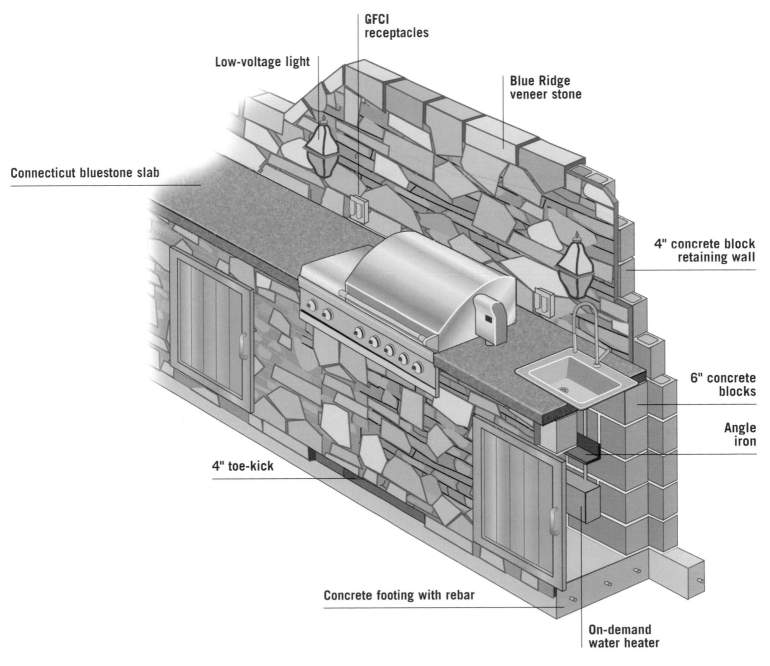

Low-voltage light

GFCI receptacles

Blue Ridge veneer stone

Connecticut bluestone slab

4" concrete block retaining wall

6" concrete blocks

Angle iron

4" toe-kick

Concrete footing with rebar

On-demand water heater

Kate Stickley,
Arterra Landscape
Architects;
Siteworks,
landscape
contractor

Landscape architect Kate Stickley was asked to create a brick terrace off the back of a traditional-style home that would serve as an area in which to eat and gather and would hide the view of the driveway from inside the house. The solution was a midsized counter and a painted arbor that blends with the house yet defines an outdoor living space.

Design

The main feature of this outdoor kitchen is the glazed ceramic tile that beautifully ties together the green and terra-cotta colors of the patio and house. The homeowners chose the design based on tiles seen on a trip to Portugal. Brick surrounds the concrete block structure and visually anchors the counter to the patio.

can I do this?

This project requires plumbing, gas, and electrical work. Hire a contractor for those tasks and spend your time mastering the brick wall and the tiling.

DEGREE OF DIFFICULTY

1   2   **3**   4   5
(moderate)

WHAT YOU'LL NEED

Grill	Concrete for the footing	2 x 4s and 2 x 2s to build forms for the countertop
Side burner	Concrete blocks	Concrete and reinforcing bar for the countertop
Refrigerator	Steel reinforcing bar	
Tile	Metal wall ties	Magnesium float
Bricks	Mortar mix	Hammer and nails
Metal doors	Angle iron	Concrete edger
Gas pipe, shutoff valve, and connections	Metal wall ties	Wet saw
Electrical supplies: cable or conduit with wire, boxes, GFCI receptacles	Hammer drill with masonry bit	Thinset mortar
	Masonry screws	Fortified grout
Plumbing supplies: supply line, drain line, stop valve	½" concrete backerboard	Square-notched trowel
		Grout sealer

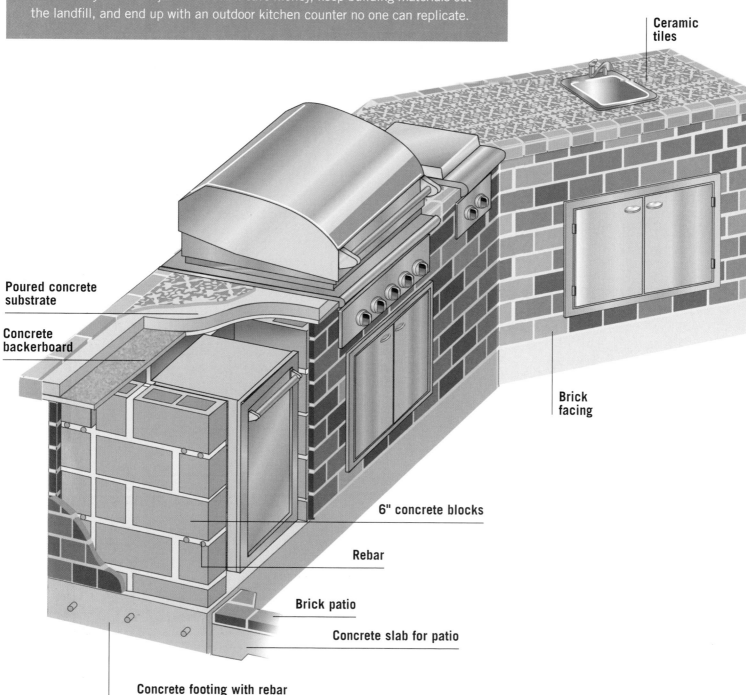

Ceramic tiles

Poured concrete substrate

Concrete backerboard

Brick facing

6" concrete blocks

Rebar

Brick patio

Concrete slab for patio

Concrete footing with rebar

BUILDING THE KITCHEN

❶ Excavate, Run the Lines, and Pour the Concrete

Excavate and build forms for a concrete footing that will meet local building codes with respect to such considerations as the depth of the footing and the size and spacing of the steel reinforcing bar. Hire contractors to run plumbing lines for the sink and a gas line with shutoff, per local codes, positioned so that the lines will enter inside the counter (see pages 100–101). You will need gas lines for the grill and side burner and electricity for the GFCI-rated receptacles and refrigerator. If needed, install steel reinforcements in the footing and vertical rebar that will run up through the cells of the blocks. Pour and finish the footing.

❷ Build the Block Walls

After allowing the footing to cure for several days, build the block walls (see pages 106–109). Six-inch concrete blocks were used for the walls, and steel reinforcing bar extends through every other opening. Because these walls will be faced with brick, embed metal wall ties in the mortar between courses of concrete blocks every 16 inches vertically. These will help secure the bricks to the concrete blocks. Have your contractor run electrical conduit through the blocks for the receptacle on the face of the counter (see pages 136–137). Use angle iron to support the blocks that span the doorways and check to be sure that the doors and appliances will fit. Then fill the cells with concrete.

❸ Frame and Pour the Countertop Substrate

See pages 130–133 for instructions on pouring a concrete countertop. Cut pieces of concrete backerboard to fit, set them in place, and make sure the grill and burner will fit in the openings. Use mortar or construction adhesive to attach the ½-inch concrete backerboard to the top of the block walls. Inside the counter, prop boards to support the backerboard while you pour. Construct a form for the concrete using 2 x 4s and 2 x 2s. Add reinforcing mesh or a grid of rebar that will run through the center of the countertop's thickness. Mix concrete and pour it into the form, trowel the surface smooth, and later remove the boards and trowel the edges. Allow the concrete to cure slowly.

❹ Lay the Bricks

See pages 110–113 for instructions on building a brick wall. Spread mortar onto a bottom corner of the concrete block wall and press the bricks into the mortar. Also throw a line of mortar on top of each brick so they will all be connected to one another and to the block wall via the metal wall ties. Strike and clean the joints as you go. Every few rows, measure up from the concrete slab and check with a level to make sure you are maintaining straight lines.

❺ Set the Tiles

Lay countertop tiles following the instructions on pages 126–129. Dry-lay the tiles, make cuts as necessary, then lay one section at a time in thinset mortar. Set the field tiles first, then tile the edges. Wait a day or two for the mortar to harden, then apply grout and wipe the surface clean. Seal the grout once it has cured.

❻ Install the Appliances and Doors

Hire a contractor to hook up the receptacles and install flexible lines from the gas shutoff (see pages 134–137) that will reach the grill and side burner. Attach the faucet and trap to the sink, set the sink, and make the plumbing connections (see pages 138–141). Then install all of the appliances and doors per the manufacturers' instructions (see pages 142–143).

LEFT: Hand-painted ceramic tiles add personal style to this outdoor kitchen.

RIGHT: A side burner was tucked into this inside corner, making the measurements for the opening very important for laying the brick facing and tile.

midcentury modern

Mara Young,
landscape
architect; Charles
Smith, Gentry
Landscapes; Geri
Martin Wilson

andscape Architect Mara Young and her client designed this outdoor kitchen adjacent to a 1950s Eichler home. The aesthetic inside the home was extended to the outdoor kitchen to create a seamless indoor-outdoor space. Young achieved this by being consistent with her materials, using granite and slate for the outdoor kitchen's countertop and back-splash, and tinting the concrete paving to coordinate with the colors of the house.

Design

Building the outdoor kitchen along an exterior wall of the house meant contractor Charles Smith could tap into the gas line of the interior fireplace for the grill and burner. The chimney outside the house was originally brick, but it was covered with multicolored slate tiles as a backsplash to draw the eye to the grill and coordinate with slate on the patio. A narrow window was installed at one end of the counter to pass food and dishes from the main kitchen.

can I do this?

Building against the main house makes plumbing and electrical connections less expensive, and applying wood siding is not difficult. This design was complicated by the wrap around the exterior chimney.

DEGREE OF DIFFICULTY

1 **2** 3 4 5
(moderate)

WHAT YOU'LL NEED

Grill	Plumbing supplies: drain line, supply line, stop valve	Masonry screws
Side burner		Wood putty
Sink with faucet and trap	Concrete for the footing	½" concrete backerboard
Outdoor siding	Concrete block	Exterior plywood
Exterior paint	Steel reinforcing bar	Wet saw
Slab of granite	Mortar mix	Thinset mortar
Slate tiles	Angle iron	Fortified grout
Gas pipe, shutoff valve, and connections	Aluminum flashing	Grout sealer
Electrical supplies: cable or conduit with wire, boxes, GFCI receptacle	Pressure-treated 2 x 4 lumber	Stone sealer
	Masonry anchors	Silicone caulk

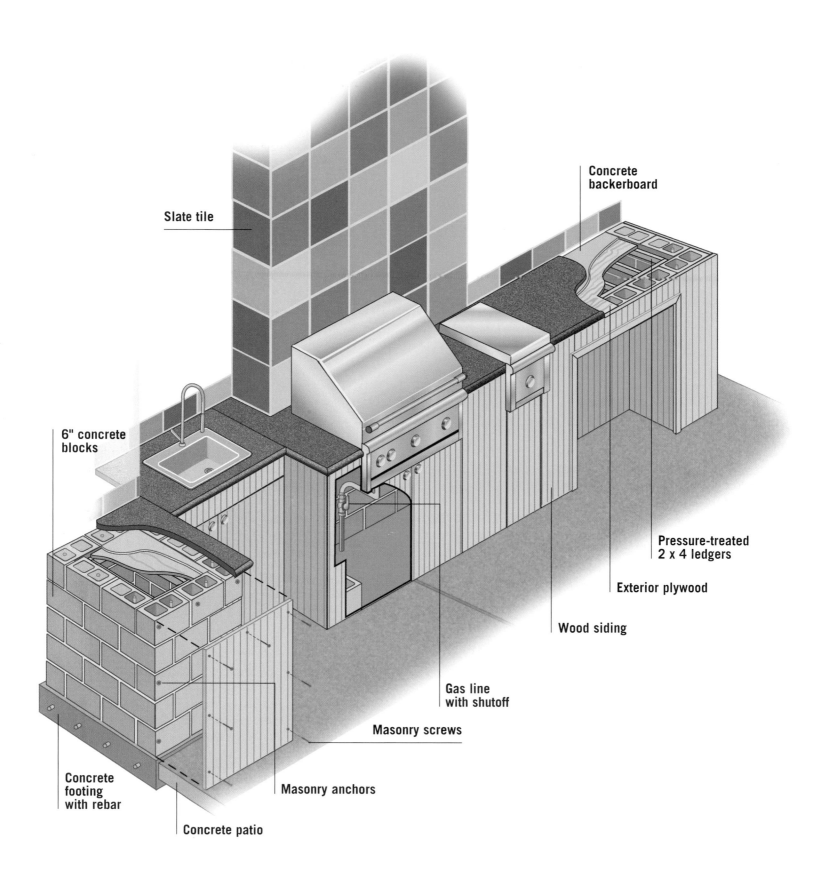

Concrete backerboard

Slate tile

6" concrete blocks

Pressure-treated 2 x 4 ledgers

Exterior plywood

Wood siding

Gas line with shutoff

Masonry screws

Concrete footing with rebar

Masonry anchors

Concrete patio

BUILDING THE KITCHEN

1 Excavate, Run the Lines, and Pour the Concrete

Excavate and build forms for a concrete footing that will meet local building codes with respect to such considerations as the depth of the footing and the size and spacing of the steel reinforcing bar. Hire contractors to run the gas line with a shutoff, per local codes, positioned so that the line will enter inside the counter and to lay electrical conduit (see pages 100–101). If needed, install steel reinforcements in the footing and vertical rebar that will run up through the cells of the blocks. Pour and finish the footing.

2 Build the Block Walls

After allowing the slab to cure for several days, build the block walls (see pages 106–109). This contractor used 6-inch concrete block for the walls with No. 4 rebar every 18 inches, and he filled the voids with concrete. He also installed aluminum flashing between the counter and the existing house siding. Have your contractor run electrical conduit through the blocks for the receptacle on the face of the counter (see pages 136–137). Use angle iron to support the blocks that span the doorways and check to be sure that the doors and appliances will fit. Then fill the cells with concrete.

3 Apply the Countertop Substrate

In this project, the contractor cut pieces of pressure-treated 2 x 4s to create horizontal ledgers around the inside edge of the concrete block. He stopped short of the area around the grill and the side burner, as those particular models could sit directly on the concrete block and wood should never touch the cooking equipment. Use masonry anchors and screws to hold each end of the ledgers in place. Then cut and screw in pressure-treated studs running between the ledger pieces every 12 inches. Once the frame is in place, cut pieces of ¾-inch exterior plywood to fit, then screw them into the wooden frame. Check that the cooking units will fit in the cutouts you made in the plywood, then cut matching pieces of ½-inch concrete backerboard and screw that to the plywood below. Alternatively, you can pour a concrete substrate to support the stone (see pages 130–133), or the stone may be installed directly over the concrete block walls. Check with your stone fabricator for the substrate needed.

4 Apply the Siding

If you live in a wet climate, seal the concrete block walls before applying wood siding so that moisture retained in the concrete will not cause the wood to rot. Cut pieces of siding to size. Use a hammer drill to make pilot holes through the wood siding and into the concrete block. Take the siding off and push the sleeve anchor into the hole. Put the siding back up, align the two holes, and use a drill to drive masonry screws into the anchors. The siding should be anchored with screws every 6 inches where there is concrete block to drill into. Countersink the screws and fill in the holes with wood putty before priming and painting.

5 Have the Granite Countertop Installed

Once the walls are built, you can have a stone fabricator come out and produce a template for the granite countertop. You will need to have the appliances and sink on site for the templating appointment so properly sized holes can be made. It might take a week or two between the fabrication appointment and installation.

6 Tile the Backsplash

Apply a layer of aluminum flashing over the existing exterior siding and secure it with masonry screws. Lay out the tile design on paper first, make any cuts with a wet saw, and lay the tiles over thinset mortar. When all tiles are set and the mortar has cured, grout the tiles. Seal the gap between the backsplash and the countertop, and between the quarter-round at the top of the backsplash and the siding, with a thick bead of silicone caulk.

7 Install the Appliances and Doors

Hire a contractor to hook up the receptacles and install flexible lines from the gas shutoff (see pages 134–137). Then set and install the grill and side burner per the manufacturers' instructions (see pages 142–143). Hook up the sink and faucet to the water supply and drainpipes that were roughed in at the start (see pages 138–141). Then attach the doors. Once the grout on the tiles has cured, apply two coats of sealant to the tiles and the granite countertop.

corner
kitchen

Kate Stickley, Arterra Landscape Architects; Kevin Brush, contractor; Elements Landscape

U nder the canopy of redwood trees, this modern
outdoor kitchen is designed in two L-shaped
sections, which provide plenty of space for meal
preparation and entertaining. The siding is sustainably
harvested ipe. While wood siding can be easily attached
to a wood-framed structure, this project used wood
framing only for the counter that abuts a concrete block
retaining wall. The other counter was made of concrete
block to provide needed strength for a stand-alone
structure on this sloping lot. The instructions on the following pages describe the procedure for constructing both
wood-framed and concrete block counters, but in your
own project, you will likely choose one or the other.

Design

Topping the 6-foot pieces of horizontal ipe siding are green granite
countertops. All materials used in the backyard—stone, wood, and concrete—continue the contemporary character of surrounding garden
rooms. The bar counter defines the work space and gives an edge to
the adjacent dining area, while the back counter nestles into the hillside.

can I do this?

If you have basic wood-
working skills, building
a wood-framed structure
and adding wood siding
can be less cumbersome
than constructing a
concrete block wall.
Hire a contractor for the
gas, electric, and
plumbing lines.

DEGREE OF DIFFICULTY

1   2   **3**   4   5
(moderate)

WOOD-FRAMED COUNTER

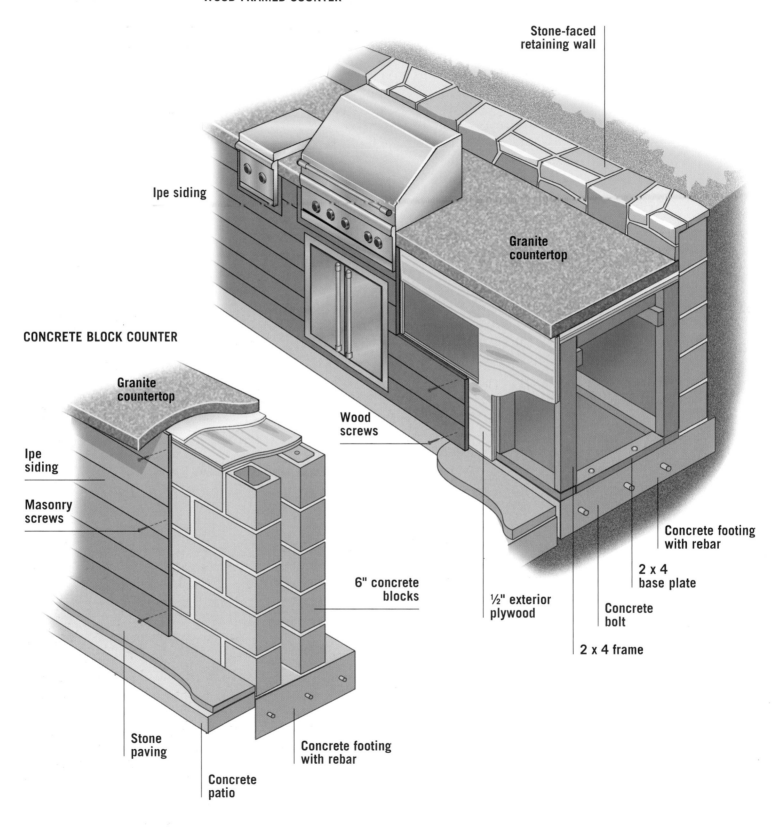

Stone-faced
retaining wall

Ipe siding

Granite
countertop

Wood
screws

CONCRETE BLOCK COUNTER

Granite
countertop

Ipe
siding

Masonry
screws

6" concrete
blocks

Concrete footing
with rebar

2 x 4
base plate

½" exterior
plywood

Concrete
bolt

2 x 4 frame

Stone
paving

Concrete footing
with rebar

Concrete
patio

WHAT YOU'LL NEED

Grill

Side burner

Refrigerator

Sink with faucet and trap

3" x 6' Ipe siding

Granite slab

Metal doors

Gas pipe, shutoff valve, and connections

Electrical supplies: cable or conduit with wire, boxes, GFCI receptacles

Plumbing supplies: supply line, drain line, stop valve

Concrete for the footing

Concrete blocks

Steel reinforcing bar

Mortar mix

Angle iron

Hammer drill with masonry bit

Masonry screws and anchors

½" concrete backerboard or exterior plywood

Drill with bits

Wood screws

Pressure-treated 2 x 4s

Circular saw or power miter box

Family and friends can sit at the bar counter to enjoy the view and eat appetizers.

BUILDING THE KITCHEN

❶ Excavate, Run the Lines, and Pour the Concrete

Excavate and build forms for a concrete footing that will meet local building codes with respect to such considerations as the depth of the footing and the size and spacing of the steel reinforcing bar. Hire contractors to run plumbing lines for the sink and a gas line with shutoff, per local codes, positioned so that they will enter inside the counter (see pages 100–101). You'll need gas lines for the grill and side burner and electricity for the GFCI-rated receptacles, refrigerator, and warming drawer. If needed, install steel reinforcements in the footing and vertical rebar that will run up through the cells of the blocks. Pour and finish the footing. A wood-framed counter does not always require a concrete footing, but in this case one was made to hold the weight of the solid stone countertop.

❷ Build the Block Counter

After allowing the footing to cure for several days, build the block walls (see pages 106–109). Six-inch concrete blocks were used for the walls, and steel reinforcing bar extends through every other opening. Have your contractor run electrical conduit through the blocks for the receptacle on the face of the counter (see pages 136–137). Use lengths of angle iron to support the blocks that span the doorways and check to be sure that the doors and appliances will fit. Then fill the cells with concrete. Cut pieces of ½-inch exterior plywood and use mortar or construction adhesive to secure it to the tops of the concrete block walls, creating a subbase for the stone countertop. The ipe siding will hide the edge of the plywood.

❸ Build the Wooden Counter

See pages 116–117 for instructions on constructing a wood-framed counter. Using concrete anchors and bolts, anchor the 2 x 4 base plates to the concrete footing. Once the frame is built, cut and screw in pieces of concrete backerboard to close in each side. Cut holes for appliances and test to make sure they fit. In this project, ½-inch exterior plywood was used instead of backerboard, but this is advisable only in very dry climates.

❹ Apply the Countertop Substrate

Cut pressure-treated 2 x 4s to span the opening of the counter every 12 inches, except under the grill and the side burner. In this example, those appliances sit directly on the concrete block. Use masonry screws and metal brackets to hold both ends of the joists in place. Then cut pieces of ¾-inch marine-grade plywood to fit and anchor them to the wooden joists with screws. Check that the cooking units will fit in the cutouts you made in the plywood, then cut matching pieces of ½-inch backerboard and screw them to the plywood below. Now you have a solid base for the countertop.

SUNSET MARKET EDITOR
JESS CHAMBERLAIN ON

sustainably harvested wood

❯❯ Ipe siding is an ideal choice for an outdoor kitchen counter because it's naturally resistant to mold, rotting, and insects. It's also incredibly hard and dense, making ipe difficult to scratch or dent. Especially with tropical hardwoods, it's important to buy Forest Stewardship Council (FSC) certified material. This certification ensures that strict environmental standards were followed when the wood was cultivated, harvested, and milled.

❺ Apply the Siding

If you live in a wet climate, seal the concrete block walls before applying wood siding so that moisture retained in the concrete will not cause the wood to rot. Starting with the bottom row, use masonry screws to attach the ipe siding to the concrete block counter and wood screws to attach the siding to the wood-framed counter. To make sure your lines stay straight and even, use a level to mark both ends of each piece on the exterior plywood or concrete backerboard before you screw them in. Follow the grill and side burner manufacturers' instructions regarding minimum clearances between wood and the appliances.

❻ Have the Granite Countertop Installed

Once the walls are built, you can have a stone fabricator come out and produce a template for the granite countertop. You will need to have the appliances and sink on site for the templating appointment so properly sized holes can be made. It might take a week or two between the fabrication appointment and installation.

❼ Install the Appliances and Doors

Have a contractor hook up the receptacles and install flexible lines from the gas shutoff (see pages 134–137) that will reach the grill and the side burner. Attach the faucet and trap to the sink, set the sink, and make the plumbing connections (see pages 138–141). Then install all of the appliances and doors per the manufacturers' instructions (see pages 142–143).

BOTTOM LEFT: Rough-edged granite, richly colored ipe, and shiny stainless steel make a gorgeous combination.

BOTTOM RIGHT: A full-size sink provides plenty of space for meal preparation and cleanup.

down-home barbecue

Don Modica, Modica Landscaping; Hernandez Welding

The design of this spacious and rustic outdoor kitchen was a collaboration between the home-owners and their longtime landscape contractor, Don Modica. With a big family that loves to entertain, they needed something that could handle everything from Sunday dinners to cooking large quantities of barbecue for local school and church functions. The result is a place that brings their adult children home and friends and neighbors over every time they light a fire for pizza or barbecue.

Design

To give the design a rustic and weathered feel, the builders interspersed the brick siding with rough stones. In front of the counter is a herringbone-pattern sand-laid brick patio. The countertop is constructed of large pieces of Connecticut bluestone that were cut to fit and mortared to a poured concrete substrate. Instead of buying a stainless-steel grill, the homeowners commissioned a custom charcoal barbecue. The pizza oven insert was framed out and topped with a slate roof.

can I do this?

Framing a large masonry structure and building a roof for the chimney require advanced construction skills. Creating a patchwork effect with bricks and stone means lots of cutting that requires time and patience.

DEGREE OF DIFFICULTY

1   2   3   4   **5**
(difficult)

WHAT YOU'LL NEED

Charcoal barbecue

Pizza oven insert

Bricks

Fieldstone

Connecticut bluestone

Slate shingles

Low-voltage exterior lights

Electrical supplies: cable or conduit with wire, boxes, GFCI receptacles

Concrete for the footing

Concrete blocks

½" concrete backerboard

Steel reinforcing bar

Metal wall ties

Mortar mix

Mortar bag

Angle iron

Hammer

Cold chisel

Trowel

Roofing materials

Spark arrester

Chimney cap

2 x 4s and 2 x 2s for the substrate framing

Concrete for the substrate

Level

BUILDING THE KITCHEN

❶ Excavate, Run the Lines, and Pour the Concrete

Excavate and build forms for a concrete footing that will meet local building codes with respect to such considerations as the depth of the footing and the size and spacing of the steel reinforcing bar. Hire a contractor to run electrical lines for the GFCI-rated receptacles (see pages 100–101). If needed, install steel reinforcements in the footing and vertical rebar that will run up through the cells of the blocks. Pour and finish the footing.

❷ Build the Block Walls

After allowing the footing to cure for several days, build the block walls (see pages 106–109). Six-inch concrete blocks were used for the walls, and steel reinforcing bar extends through every other opening. Because these walls will be faced with brick and stone, embed metal wall ties in the mortar between courses of concrete blocks every 16 inches vertically as you build. Run electrical conduit through the blocks for the receptacles on the face of the counter (see pages 136–137). Use angle iron to support the blocks that span the doorways. Custom iron doors were built for this project, but if you buy pre-made doors, make sure they will fit in the openings you create. Then fill the cells with concrete.

❸ Install the Pizza Oven

The homeowners purchased a Medio 110 pizza oven from Mugnaini. Follow the manu-facturer's instructions carefully to install the kit on top of the concrete block base.

❹ Build the Pizza Oven Surround and Roof

Continue building concrete block walls around the pizza oven insert, which is fully enclosed with a concrete backerboard sur-round. Then have your contractor frame the roof over the concrete block wall. Consult a contractor or roofing manual to build a fire-safe roof. The roof in this example was finished with slate shingles. Be sure to equip the chimney with a spark arrester and cap.

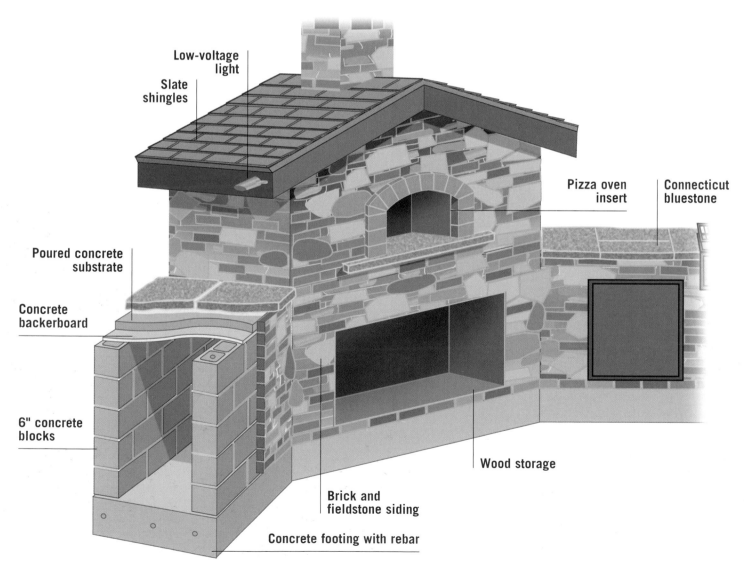

Low-voltage light

Slate shingles

Poured concrete substrate

Concrete backerboard

6" concrete blocks

Pizza oven insert

Connecticut bluestone

Wood storage

Brick and fieldstone siding

Concrete footing with rebar

⑤ Frame and Pour the Countertop Substrate

See pages 130–133 for instructions on pouring a concrete countertop. Cut pieces of concrete backerboard to fit, set them in place, and make sure the barbecue will fit in the opening. For this design, the concrete substrate was run to the outside edges of the concrete block walls. The edges of the substrate will later be concealed by the brick siding. Use mortar or construction adhesive to attach the ½-inch concrete backerboard to the top of the concrete block walls. Inside the counter, prop boards to support the backerboard while you pour. Construct a form for the concrete using 2 x 4s and 2 x 2s. Add reinforcing mesh or a grid of rebar that will run through the center of the countertop's thickness. Mix concrete and pour it into the form, trowel the surface smooth, and later remove the form boards and trowel the edges. Allow the concrete to cure slowly.

⑥ Apply the Siding

See pages 110–113 for instructions on building a brick wall. Use the metal ties you installed when you built the concrete block wall to support the brick wall. Strike and clean the joints as you go. Every few rows, measure up from the concrete slab and check with a level to make sure you are maintaining straight lines. In this example, fieldstones were placed intermittently throughout the design. The masons selected randomly sized stones and mortared each one in place, then cut bricks to wrap around them.

⑦ Install the Countertop

Follow the instructions on pages 122–123 and 126–129 for installing stone or tile on a countertop. Select large pieces of Connecticut bluestone and test them for fit in a dry run over the concrete substrate. Use a hammer and cold chisel to cut them into randomly shaped pieces. When you're happy with the configuration, mortar each piece onto the concrete substrate. Use a mortar bag to fill in the joints with additional mortar and wipe the stones clean.

⑧ Install the Barbecue and Doors

Hook up the receptacles (see pages 136–137). Install the barbecue and doors. In this example, both components were custom made. If you use a stock barbecue or doors, be sure to consult the manufacturers' instructions regarding installation. Install the low-voltage lights on the fascia.

LEFT: A Connecticut bluestone hearth outside the pizza oven visually connects with the flanking countertops and provides a surface on which to rest the pizza when it's done cooking.

RIGHT: This custom charcoal barbecue offers plenty of cooking surface for large parties. Crank up one side so fish and veggies get less heat while the other side stays low to cook meats at a higher temperature.

Keith Willig
Landscape
Architecture and
Construction

A stunning hillside setting makes this a popular backyard for cooking and entertaining, but the same hill also created many construction issues for landscape architect Keith Willig and his crew. "It took a year to get the permits to build it with all of the soil and drainage tests that needed to be done," he explains. But if you took the same design and placed it on a level patio, it would not be a terribly difficult project, because it features a charcoal grill and pizza oven kit, neither of which requires a gas line. Willig did run electricity out to the kitchen, however, burying the chase pipes under a new concrete patio.

Design

The homeowners wanted a stucco finish to match the house in color and texture, but they added architectural stone veneer from Eldorado Stone around the base of the pizza oven. Custom-made redwood doors and water-washed, randomly shaped Connecticut bluestone pieces on the countertop give the outdoor kitchen a rustic feel.

can I do this?

Special touches like the custom doors and a pizza oven kit will be challenging for novice builders, but veneer stone facing and a stand-alone charcoal grill make other parts of the design easier.

DEGREE OF DIFFICULTY

1 2 3 **4** 5
(moderate)

WHAT YOU'LL NEED

Charcoal grill

Stucco mix

Connecticut bluestone flagstones

Custom redwood doors

Veneer stone

Pizza oven kit

Electrical supplies: cable or conduit with wire, boxes, GFCI receptacle

Concrete for the footing

Concrete blocks

Steel reinforcing bar

Mortar mix

Angle iron

Hammer drill with masonry bit

Masonry screws

½" concrete backerboard

2 x 4s

Concrete and reinforcing bar for the countertop

Thinset mortar

Square-notched trowel

Mortar bag

BUILDING THE KITCHEN

❶ Excavate, Run Electrical Lines, and Pour the Concrete

Excavate and build forms for a concrete footing that will meet local building codes with respect to such considerations as the depth of the footing and the size and spacing of the steel reinforcing bar. Hire a contractor to run electrical wires for the GFCI-rated receptacles (see pages 100–101). If needed, install steel reinforcements in the footing and vertical rebar that will run up through the cells of the blocks.

❷ Build the Block Walls

After allowing the footing to cure for several days, build the block walls (see pages 106–109). Because of the hill in this project, the back wall ties into a retaining wall and required 8-inch concrete blocks, while the front and side walls were constructed of 6-inch concrete blocks. Both walls are tied to the concrete footing with steel reinforcing bars that extend through every other concrete block opening. Have your contractor run electrical conduit through the blocks for the receptacle on the face of the counter (see pages 136–137). Use angle iron to support the blocks that span the openings and check to be sure that the doors and appliances will fit. Then fill the cells with concrete.

❸ Build the Countertop Substrate

A 3-inch internal concrete slab was poured to support the countertop. On top of short concrete block walls inside the structure, cut and lay pieces of ½-inch concrete backerboard so that the top of the pieces sits 3 inches below the top of the exterior concrete block walls; attach with mortar or construction adhesive. Temporarily support any spans longer than 12 inches with plywood and vertical 2 x 4s. Add steel reinforcement and pour a slab (see pages 130–133). If your grill requires a solid support, include the concrete substrate underneath it as well (see pages 98–99); if not, you can stop short of the grill. Remove the temporary plywood and 2 x 4 supports once the slab has cured.

❹ Stucco

Apply two or three coats of stucco to each side of the counter (see pages 120–121). You can either apply a finish coat of stucco with integral color, or paint the stucco after it has fully cured. If you're trying to match the texture of the house or a nearby wall, practice on a scrap of concrete backerboard until you master the technique. Then install the outside electrical receptacle.

A large wood-storage area under the pizza oven keeps fuel close at hand.

⑤ Apply the Veneer Stone

Follow the instructions on page 119 to set the Eldorado stone veneer. Spread mortar over the block wall and set stones in place using the manufacturer's drawings as guidance. Let the mortar harden, then use a mortar bag to fill the joints. In this project, the joints were raked after installation so that the mortar is far back in the grooves, making it look like a dry-stacked stone wall.

⑥ Set the Stone Countertop

Lay the randomly shaped Connecticut bluestone pieces following the instructions on pages 122–123 and 126–129. Lay out stones in a dry run, make cuts as necessary using a hammer and cold chisel, then lay one section at a time in thinset mortar. Wait a day or two for the mortar to harden, then use a mortar bag to fill wide joints with additional mortar. Seal the entire stone countertop several times once the mortar is cured.

⑦ Build the Pizza Oven

This project used the Medio 100 model from Mugnaini. The kit includes floor and crown elements, the exhaust and insulation, and an iron door. Follow the manufacturers' step-by-step installation guide or hire a professional to build this structure.

⑧ Install the Appliances and Doors

Hook up the receptacles (see pages 136–137). Set and install the charcoal grill per the manufacturer's instructions (see pages 142–143). Install the redwood doors.

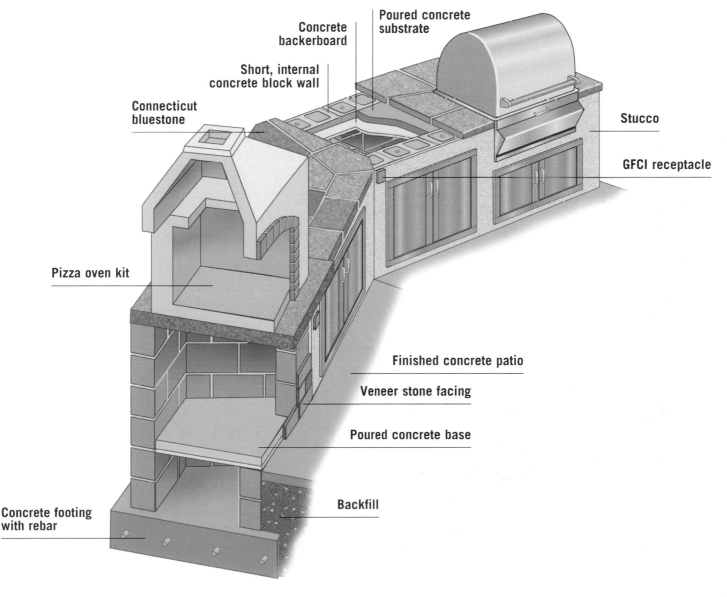

- Concrete backerboard
- Poured concrete substrate
- Short, internal concrete block wall
- Connecticut bluestone
- Stucco
- GFCI receptacle
- Pizza oven kit
- Finished concrete patio
- Veneer stone facing
- Poured concrete base
- Backfill
- Concrete footing with rebar

homestead kitchen

Landscape architect Vera Gates created an agrarian garden around legacy oak trees, maintaining the integrity of the land for a young and active family. Food production is an integral part of the design, from vegetable gardens to orchards of fruit trees, culminating in the full outdoor kitchen just steps from the house. A low gas fire pit ties into the outdoor kitchen and warms up the dining area. The outdoor kitchen includes both gas and charcoal grills, a sink, and a refrigerator.

Design

In keeping with the farmhouse aesthetic of the home and garden, Gates used a combination of Bitterroot and Canyon Creek ledger stones to face the outdoor kitchen counter. Warm brown and terra-cotta tones bridge the speckled gray granite countertop and bluestone pavers on the terrace. The same stones were used to face a 10-inch backsplash. The arbor and access doors were painted white to match the house. A raised countertop on metal legs creates additional space for eating or serving.

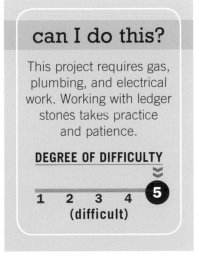

can I do this?

This project requires gas, plumbing, and electrical work. Working with ledger stones takes practice and patience.

DEGREE OF DIFFICULTY

1   2   3   4   **5**
(difficult)

WHAT YOU'LL NEED

Gas grill

Charcoal grill

Icemaker

Refrigerator

Sink with faucet and trap

Granite slab

Ledger stones

Custom wooden doors

Custom metal legs

Gas pipe, shutoff valve, and connections

Electrical supplies: cable or conduit with wire, boxes, GFCI receptacle

Plumbing supplies: supply line, drain line, stop valve

Concrete for the footing

Concrete blocks

Steel reinforcing bar

Metal wall ties

Mortar mix

Angle iron

Hammer

Cold chisel

Trowel

BUILDING THE KITCHEN

❶ Excavate, Run the Lines, and Pour the Concrete

Excavate and build forms for a concrete footing that will meet local building codes with respect to such considerations as the depth of the footing and the size and spacing of the steel reinforcing bar. Hire a contractor to run the gas line with a shutoff, per local codes, positioned so that it will enter inside the counter (see pages 100–101). Run plumbing lines for the sink and electrical lines for the icemaker, refrigerator, and GFCI-rated receptacles. If needed, install steel reinforcements in the footing and vertical rebar that will run up through the cells of the blocks. Pour and finish the footing.

❷ Build the Block Walls

After allowing the footing to cure for several days, build the block walls (see pages 106–109). Six-inch concrete blocks were used for the walls, and steel reinforcing bar extends through every other opening. Because these walls will be faced with stone, embed metal wall ties in the mortar between courses of concrete blocks every 16 inches vertically as you build. Four-inch concrete blocks were used to create the structure for the stone-faced backsplash on two sides of the counter. Internal block walls run perpendicular to the exterior walls on either side of the charcoal grill, in the corners, and on either side of the gas grill, creating extra support for these appliances and the stone countertop. Have your contractor run electrical conduit through the blocks for the receptacles on the face of the counter and backsplash (see pages 136–137). Use angle iron to support the blocks that span the doorways and check to be sure that the doors and appliances will fit. Then fill the cells with concrete.

❸ Install the Ledger Stones

Following the instructions on pages 122–123, set the ledger stones. These stones are thicker than flagstones and much heavier than man-made veneer stones. Starting at a bottom corner, skim-coat a small area of concrete block wall with mortar. Set stones carefully, aiming for an irregular pattern of shapes and colors. Use a hammer and cold chisel to shape stones as needed. Stack them close if you want to achieve a dry-laid appearance, as was done on this project. Back-butter each stone and rake the joints as you go to keep the mortar deep within the joints.

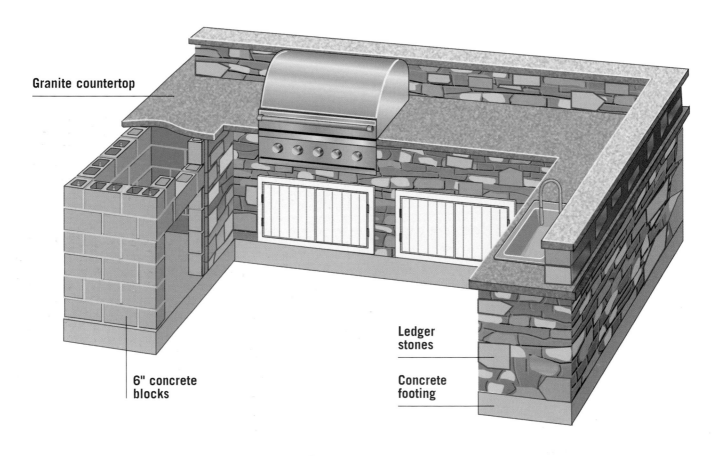

Granite countertop

Ledger stones

6" concrete blocks

Concrete footing

④ Have the Granite Countertop Installed

Once the walls are built, you can have a stone fabricator come out and produce a template for the granite countertop. You will need to have the appliances and sink on site for the templating appointment so properly sized holes can be made. It might take a week or two between the fabrication appointment and installation. Because of the multiple interior block walls in this project, the stone has enough support and doesn't require a substrate.

⑤ Finish the Backsplash

After the granite is installed on the countertop and the top of the backsplash, fill in the remaining space with ledger stones as you did on the counter below. Work around the GFCI-rated receptacles that were brought up through the stone blocks. Again, rake the joints so that the mortar stays deep within them for the appearance of dry-stacked stone.

⑥ Install the Appliances and Doors

Hire a contractor to hook up the receptacles and install flexible lines from the gas shutoff (see pages 134–137). Then set and install the grills and refrigerator per the manufacturers' instructions (see pages 142–143). Hook up the sink and faucet to the water supply and drainpipes that were roughed in at the start (see pages 138–141).

LEFT: Undermount sinks allow you to wipe debris straight in. Self-rimming sinks don't require edges, but the outside edge of the sink sitting on the countertop will be difficult to keep clean.

RIGHT: Rake the mortar joints with a fine-pointed tool to achieve this look of a dry-stacked wall.

your tools

Do-it-yourselfers may need to add a few pieces to their tool collection. What you need will depend on the complexity of the structure you plan to build, and on whether you're doing any of your own plumbing and electrical work or subbing those parts of the project out. Below is a selection of the tools you may need to have on hand.

FRAMING SQUARE

PROPANE TORCH

CONCRETE EDGER

MARGIN TROWEL

WIRE STRIPPERS

SNAP CUTTER

DRILL

LAMINATED GROUT FLOAT

LEVEL

CAULK GUN

RUBBER MALLET

MASON'S CORNER BLOCKS

TUBING CUTTER

LINEMAN'S PLIERS

MASON'S TROWEL

NOTCHED TROWEL

TESTER

CHALK LINE

PVC SAW

PVC CUTTERS

MAGNESIUM FLOAT

SLIP-JOINT PLIERS

TAPE MEASURE

supporting the grill

An adjustable flange allows for slight movement of the grill. Once the grill is in place, seal the edge with a bead of caulk.

Shut Down
Turn gas supply off.
Turn all knobs to OFF.

W hile small, light grills can simply rest on the counter's framing, large grills often need something more. Select your grill before constructing the counter so you can add one of the support options discussed below.

Reverse-engineer the grill height so that the support you build will allow the flange of the grill to rest on the countertop. The countertop and grill height should be slightly below the elbow height of the person who will do most of the cooking. Measure the total height of the underlayment and whatever finish material—tile, concrete, stone—you plan to use for the countertop. Include about 1/8 inch for mortar if you are planning to tile. Some models have adjustable side flanges so you can adjust the height by about an inch once the unit is installed.

Some manufacturers require that the grill be installed within three solid walls and a bottom support, like this one. Before installation, holes may need to be drilled for the fuel line.

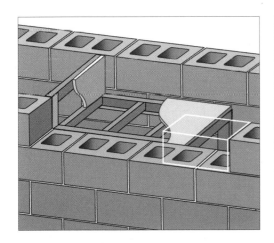

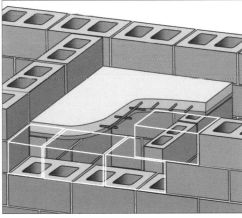

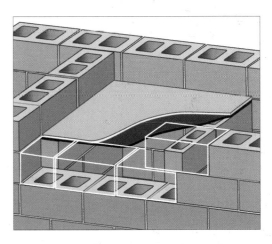

Metal Framing and Backerboard

See pages 114–115 for instructions on building with metal framing. Attach vertical and horizontal channels to the inside front and rear concrete block walls using masonry screws. Cut and attach metal joists between the channels. Then cut and screw 1/2-inch concrete backerboard into the top of the framing. Once the backerboard is attached, the structure will be plenty strong to support the grill. You can also build the walls of the counter in this way, without the concrete blocks.

Poured Concrete and Block

See pages 106–109 for instructions on building with concrete blocks. Within the opening of the counter, construct block walls abutting the exterior walls to support the concrete slab. Cut a piece of backerboard to size and lay it over the block walls. Put a piece of plywood supported by two vertical 2 x 4s underneath the 1/2-inch backerboard to temporarily hold up the concrete slab. Add steel reinforcement to the top of the backerboard, and pour a slab (see pages 130–133). Remove the wood forms once the slab has cured.

Steel Plate

Build block walls similar to those for a concrete-slab substrate (left). Purchase a sheet of 1/4-inch steel from a metal shop, lay it over the block walls, and add a layer of 1/2-inch concrete backerboard.

installing utility lines

Depending on the scope of your outdoor kitchen, you may need a gas line, conduit for electrical wiring, a water supply pipe, and a water drain line. Digging trenches out to the right spot in the yard and connecting to the main gas, water, and electric lines of the house are best left to professionals who can work in accordance with your local building codes. But skilled do-it-yourselfers sometimes choose to make their own final hookups at the counter.

Generally, building codes allow pipes to run in trenches 12 inches deep. Check with your local building department before you dig to ensure you will not accidentally break any existing gas, plumbing, or electric lines, and to ensure you will dig to the proper depth for your area. Drain lines must be properly sloped, and pipes may need to be protected with insulation or a layer of 2-by pressure-treated lumber.

Black ABS drainpipe, copper water supply pipe, black gas pipe, and PVC conduit for the electrical line run through this trench. In some areas with acidic soil, plastic water supply pipes should be used instead of copper. Also check local building code requirements to make sure you can place all the pipes in a single trench.

A dry well disperses drain water into the yard, which works if you limit the use of soap and keep food from going down the drain. This is considered gray water. Check local building codes to make sure you can do this in your area.

① Gas Line

Call your gas company and ask if it can install a fitting and shutoff valve to your existing gas pipe and connect the new pipe for your outdoor kitchen from there. Common choices are corrugated stainless steel wrapped with yellow vinyl, copper pipes wrapped in a protective sleeve, and black gas pipes made of steel. Black steel pipes will not rust underground. The gas company technician will cut with a pipe wrench and wrap the male ends of the pipes with yellow Teflon tape made for gas pipes before connecting the fittings. All fittings for rigid steel pipes must be installed underground, while flexible yellow gas pipe can make loose turns through the trench and has compression-type fittings that must be installed above ground.

② Wiring

Hire an electrician to make sure that the electrical requirements for your outdoor kitchen won't overload the circuit to which it will be connected. The electrician might choose to connect wiring to a nearby grounded indoor or outdoor receptacle. If this isn't possible, he or she might need to run the wiring to the service panel and connect to a new circuit breaker. Protect electrical lines by running them through PVC conduit that starts at the house, runs through the underground trenches, and emerges through the floor of the counter.

③ Water Supply Pipes

If the counter is installed against the house, the plumber may be able to connect to existing hot- and cold-water lines. For outdoor kitchens away from the house, have the plumber run a cold-water supply line that feeds an on-demand water heater under the counter of the outdoor kitchen (see page 139). Shutoff valves should be installed at the counter. People who live in areas with freezing winters must follow local codes to ensure supply pipes will not freeze and burst. Purge lines before the cold season using bleed valves at the low points of the pipe run, or an air compressor that blows water out of the lines.

④ Drain Line

Depending on your site and local codes, you may be able to run the drainpipe into the house's main drain, the municipal sewer system, or a city storm drain. Drain lines must slope consistently downhill at a rate of ¼ inch or more per foot. Check local codes to determine if your line must be vented, meaning tied to a vertical pipe that supplies air. You may also be able to simply run the line into a dry well (see photo at left). To make one, drill a grid of 1-inch holes in a 10-gallon plastic bucket. Drill a larger hole for the drainpipe toward the top of the bucket. Dig a hole about 6 inches deeper than the bucket, set the bucket in the hole, fill it with rocks, and run the drain line through a trench into the bucket. Cover with landscaping fabric, soil, and sod.

pouring a concrete slab

A counter built with concrete block and topped with a heavy slab needs the support of a concrete footing underneath.

Most concrete counters are heavy enough to require a reinforced concrete footing. These are generally 12 inches deep, but the depth can vary widely depending on climate, soil type, weight of the finished structure, and local building codes, so check with your building department to confirm that your footing will be built to code. The following project shows how to build a concrete slab. The same techniques can be used to build a deep footing. Depending on your local building codes and the structure you build, you may need to add steel reinforcing bar for extra strength in the footing. The bars can run horizontally in the footing only, or extend vertically to run through the concrete block structure. For some projects and in some areas, you may not need the reinforcing bar at all. Hire a professional to pour the footing if you have any doubts.

❶ Build the Form and Excavate

Mark the area and dig up the sod or any roots in the way. Build a 2 x 4 form for the slab and set it onto the excavated area. Make sure it's square and level. Anchor the form with stakes every few feet, driving them below the tops of the form boards. Stretch mason's corner blocks across the tops of the form to use as guides as you dig to the final depth of the slab. When you reach the bottom,

scrape instead of dig to avoid loosening the soil. Tamp soil with a hand tamper or 4 x 4, spread a few inches of compactable gravel, then tamp again. At this point, any gas pipes, water pipes, or electrical conduit should be run over the gravel to the correct location. A board-and-clamp arrangement, shown below in step 4, helps keep the pipes in place until the concrete cures.

❷ Order and Pour the Concrete

Give a concrete supplier the dimensions of your excavation. If you need more than ¾ cubic yard, ask the supplier to deliver in a ready-mix truck. For smaller amounts, you may choose to mix the concrete yourself in a wheelbarrow. Be sure you include any reinforcements required by your building codes. If the ready-mix truck can't reach the site with its chute, put down board paths for

wheelbarrows so the truck doesn't crush any sod. One person should wheel and dump the concrete in batches while the other uses a shovel to scrape and spread.

❸ Screed

Once the concrete has filled the form, set a straight 2 x 4 across the form boards and screed by dragging the board across the surface. Move the board in a sawing motion as you pull, and shovel more concrete onto low areas.

❹ Smooth

Allow time for pools of water, called bleed water or cream, to evaporate before reworking the surface with a magnesium or Teflon float. Hold the tool so that the leading edge is slightly raised and gently press down as you go. Use long, sweeping motions.

❺ Edge and Cure

Slip a mason's trowel between the form boards and the concrete and slice along the perimeter of the slab. This, plus tapping along the form boards with a hammer along their length, will eliminate air pockets that might weaken the concrete slab. Then run a concrete edging tool along the perimeter to round off the top edge. Once bleed water evaporates, smooth the surface again with the float.

Keep the concrete moist for several days by spraying it with a fine mist of water twice a day or covering the surface with plastic. The more slowly it cures, the stronger it will be. After a day or two, carefully remove the forms.

working with mortar and block

8" webbed stretcher

6" corner block

6" solid-end stretcher

4" block

Mortar mix

Half block

2" and 4" solid blocks

Ladder-type reinforcement

Angle iron

Rebar

Most of the projects in this chapter were built with concrete block, which is commonly available in 4-inch, 6-inch, and 8-inch pieces. Use stretcher blocks as you build the rows, and finish the edges with corner blocks. Stretchers are available with webbed ends or solid ends. As you'll see on page 109, the openings in concrete blocks can be filled in with wet concrete, reinforced with rebar, and used to house electrical boxes. Solid blocks should be placed above and below each opening you create for doors or the grill.

MIXING MORTAR
Learn to throw like a pro.

➊ Stir It Up

Pour about one-third of a bag of mortar mix into a wheelbarrow. Add water a little at a time and mix with a mason's hoe. Don't mix more than you can use before the mortar begins to harden. The mortar must be wet enough to stick but dry enough to hold its shape and not run down the wall. You should be able to cut ridges in the mortar with a mason's trowel and have it hold its shape without becoming crumbly.

➋ Scoop It Out

Use a mason's trowel to scoop up some of the mortar and hold it upside down. The mortar should stick to the trowel for a couple of seconds before sliding off. Add a little water if the mix seems too dry, or add more mortar mix if it's too wet. But this works only when you're first mixing. If the mix starts to harden or get crumbly while you work, you must throw it out and start a new batch.

CUTTING BLOCK
Always wear your safety gear.

You'll need a high-quality circular saw fitted with a diamond blade. You can also use less expensive abrasive masonry blades, but they will need to be replaced every five blocks or so. Before you cut, make sure you're wearing a respirator, protective eyewear, earplugs, and work gloves. Run the blade slowly along one side, then turn the block over and cut the other side. If the saw heats up, take a break while it cools.

construction lesson

» An alternative approach to concrete block counters—nearly as strong as the traditional methods—is to set the bottom row in a bed of mortar and dry-stack the rest of the blocks. Then use a flat trowel to smear surface-bonding mortar onto both sides of the wall. Get the surface as smooth as possible, let it dry, then apply a second coat and finish with the facing material of your choice.

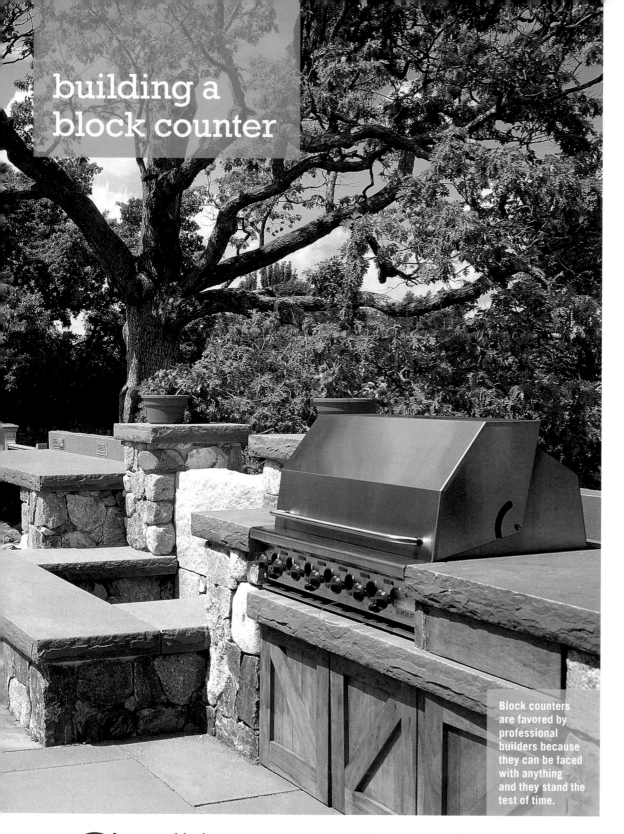

building a block counter

WHAT YOU'LL NEED

Chalk line

Type N dry mortar mix
(or type S for extra
strength or wet areas)

Wheelbarrow

Bucket

Mason's hoe

Mason's trowel
or margin trowel

Hawk

Rubber mallet

Level

Framing square

Concrete blocks

Rebar

Ladder wire (optional)

Mason's line (optional)

Angle iron

Drill with masonry bit
(optional)

Circular saw with
masonry blade (optional)

Block counters are favored by professional builders because they can be faced with anything and they stand the test of time.

Concrete block counters must rest on a firm concrete slab that is level and thick enough to satisfy local building codes. Produce a sketch of the project so you know how many and what size blocks you will need. Aim to minimize cuts by using as many full and precut half blocks as possible.

1 Spread a Bed of Mortar

Snap chalk lines and mark where each block will go. Use a framing square to check the corners. Dampen the concrete slab or footing with water, mix a batch of mortar (see page 105), and spread a ½-inch layer between the layout lines.

2 Place the first block

Set a block aligned with the end line or outside corner. You may need to scrape away some mortar to see the line. Press the block into place, check for level in both directions, and check the face of the end for plumb. Scrape away excess mortar.

3 Butter the End and Fill In

If you're building a wall that's 6 feet long or less, butter the end of the next block to form peaks as shown. Then press the stretcher block into place against the corner block. For longer walls, it's better to set up a string line and place each corner first, then fill in each row.

4 Check for Level and Plumb

Once the first row is in place, check the blocks for level. Scrape mortar onto the flanges of the laid blocks and set the next course on top. Start the second row with a corner block or half block so that the ends don't line up vertically from one row to the next. Check again that the blocks form a straight line and scrape mortar from the joints as you work.

continued on page 108

⑤ Alternative Corner Method

If you aren't using corner blocks, use a circular saw with a masonry blade to cut channels in the tops of the blocks. Bend a piece of rebar to fit in the channel, fill the cells with mortar, and set the rebar in the mortar. Do this every other course to tie the corners together.

⑥ Reinforce with Ladder Wire

To further strengthen a wall and corner, add ladder wire every other course and under the top course. Spread a layer of mortar onto the top of each row and set the wire in the mortar.

⑦ Using a Line Guide

For a long counter, set blocks at each corner and pull a mason's line taut between the two outside edges. Use the line as a guide while laying the remaining blocks of each row, and check for level and straightness.

⑧ Finishing a Long Wall

The last block to place on a long wall, called the closure block, can be tricky. If the counter isn't sized for full blocks, cut the next-to-last block and use a full block for the last one. Spread mortar on both ends, and then slide the closure block into place.

⑨ Install an Angle Iron

At the top of openings meant for doors or a refrigerator, install an angle iron to support additional rows of concrete block. Ideally, you can set it at the top of a block on each side of the opening. If not, use a circular saw equipped with a masonry blade to cut a channel in the blocks to accommodate the angle iron.

⑩ Finish the Opening

Fill the cells of the blocks on each side of the opening with concrete and set the angle iron in place. Spread mortar over the angle iron and install blocks on top.

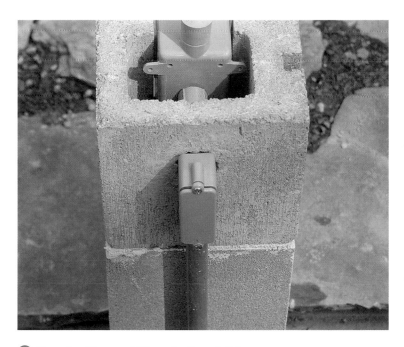

⑪ Install an Electrical Box

Whenever possible, run electrical conduit inside the counter rather than within the block cells. For an electrical box accessible on the outside of the counter, cut an opening in a concrete block and set the box so it will be flush with whatever finish option you're using. Use a masonry bit to drill several small holes and then chip out between them to create a hole for the conduit. Tap in shims around the face to wedge the box into place, then fill the block cell with concrete.

⑫ Fill the Wall for Added Strength

Pour an inch of concrete into the bottom of a cell, cut a piece of rebar an inch shorter than the height of the walls, and set it in the wet concrete. Then fill the rest of the cell with concrete. This strengthening method can be used for some or all of the cells.

Brick counters have a stately appearance. Use them to build the counter structure, or face a concrete block wall.

Like concrete block counters, brick counters must be set on a solid concrete footing or slab. If you want the facing material of your outdoor kitchen to be brick, you may choose to add a single wythe of bricks against the side of a concrete block counter. Or you can build the entire counter out of brick by using two wythes. The example on pages 112–113 shows a running-bond pattern, or two bricks over one. To tie the two wythes together, set bricks sideways for a row, called a header row, in regular intervals.

WHAT YOU'LL NEED

Type N dry mortar mix (or type S for extra strength or wet areas)

Wheelbarrow

Bucket

Mason's hoe

Mason's trowel or margin trowel

Hawk

Rubber mallet

Chalk line

Dowels

Mason's corner blocks

Pencil

Level

Framing square

Bricks

Angle iron

Circular saw with masonry blade (optional)

Jointer

Masonry brush

BRICKLAYING TECHNIQUES Master the basics of working with brick.

➊ Throw a Line of Mortar

See page 105 for instructions on mixing mortar. Scoop up some mortar with the trowel facing up, then snap the trowel downward quickly to loosen the mortar. It will make a smacking sound as it lands back on the face of the trowel. To throw the mortar, extend your arm in front of you, rotate the trowel until the mortar starts to slide off, then pull the trowel back toward you and watch the mortar hit the bricks with a slap. Deposit the mortar in an even line about 1 inch thick, ¾ brick wide, and a couple of bricks long.

➋ Furrow the Mortar

Turn the trowel on its side and drag its point through the mortar to create a channel. Don't let the mortar slide off the side of the bricks. If it does, slice the mortar as shown in step 5.

➌ Butter a Brick End

Except for the first brick in a course, each brick should have at least one buttered end. Hold a brick in one hand and spread a small amount of mortar on the trowel. Scrape the trowel at a 45-degree angle to the brick and shape each side as shown.

➍ Lay a Brick

While the mortar you threw in steps 1 and 2 is still wet, place a brick about 2 inches from the one it will abut and slide it into place. A little mortar should squeeze out the joints. If you see any gaps in the mortar greater than an inch, remove the brick, scrape away the mortar, and start again. Small gaps can be filled later.

➎ Clean Off the Excess

Hold the trowel like a knife to slice off mortar that squeezes out the sides. Slice quickly in a single motion so not much will get on the face of the bricks. Do this every 10 minutes or so.

BUILDING A DOUBLE-WYTHE WALL   Create a sturdy counter.

❶ Dry Run
Snap chalk lines on the concrete footing to indicate the perimeter of the wall and place bricks along the line. Insert ⅜- or ½-inch dowels between them to represent joints. Arrange bricks to minimize cutting. Once you have the layout set, use a pencil to mark the center of each joint and remove the dry-laid bricks.

❷ Lay the First Course
Starting at a corner, throw a line of mortar for the first few bricks. Set the corner brick, butter the end of the next one, and press against the first. Use a level every few bricks to make sure they are straight, and scrape away excess mortar as you go. Repeat for the second wythe.

❸ Lay a Header Course
Where you choose to lay a header course, you may need to cut the corner bricks, as shown. To lay a header brick, throw two lines of mortar and set bricks across the two wythes below. Scrape away excess mortar as you go and strike the joints as needed.

❹ Building a Lead
Continue building up the corner; this is referred to as building a lead. You will get the corners level and plumb, then fill in the wythes between them. Build up a corner seven or eight bricks high. Measure to ensure that the joints are the correct thickness and form regular stair steps from end to end.

⑤ String a Line Between Corners

Build up the other side as you did in the previous step. Check to see that the bricks are the same height as the ones on the opposite corner. Hook mason's corner blocks and stretch the line from one lead to the other at the center of a joint. The line should be about ⅛ inch from the corners of the bricks; do not let it touch the bricks. Be sure the line is taught.

⑥ Fill in Each Row

As you fill in each course, move the line up one joint and use it as a guide for height and to maintain a straight outer edge. The closure brick, the last brick in a course, should be buttered on both ends and slipped into place. Use a striking tool to force more mortar into this joint if needed.

⑦ Strike the Joints

As you work, test the joints by pressing them with your thumb. If the thumbprint holds its shape, it's time to strike. But if the mortar starts to harden, striking is difficult. Use a jointer to smooth the horizontal joints and then smooth the verticals.

⑧ Clean the Face of the Wall

Brush the joints with a masonry brush as soon as the mortar starts to harden. If it smears across the bricks, stop and wait a few minutes before continuing. Wipe mortar off the brick faces with a damp sponge, but do not let the mortar get wet or it will weaken.

building with metal framing

WHAT YOU'LL NEED

Metal framing channels and studs

Tin snips

Heavy work gloves

Self-tapping screws

Drill

Level

Tape measure

½" concrete backerboard

Straightedge ruler

Utility knife

Reciprocating saw or jigsaw

Concrete backerboard screws

This metal-framed structure was finished with wood siding and stone tiles for the countertop.

A lighter, less expensive way to construct an outdoor kitchen counter is to use metal framing. Build the structure with metal pieces and create solid walls with concrete backerboard, just as you'd use 2 x 4s and drywall to construct an interior wall. A metal-framed structure is fireproof, will survive freezing winters, and is light enough to rest on a well-framed deck, so you won't have to pour a thick concrete footing. Figure out the pieces you need by creating a detailed drawing of your project, but wait until you have your grill and door specifications. Studs and top cross braces should be no more than 16 inches apart.

❶ Measure and Cut

Metal framing comes in U-shaped channels and studs that fit into the channels. Factor in the thickness of the channels, ⅛ inch on each end, when measuring for cutting the studs. To make a straight cut, use tin snips on the two sides, then bend the metal back and forth until it breaks. To cut cross braces that grab at each end, cut studs 3 inches longer than the opening, then snip each end in two places and bend back two side tabs to give you three tabs that can attach to an adjoining channel or stud.

❷ Attach the Pieces

Form the bottom of the frame with channels. To accomplish this, you may need to cut one or two tabs so you can join them at the corners. Lay out the studs, then attach them by slipping them into the channels and driving self-tapping screws made for use with metal studs.

❸ Assemble the Frame

Use a helper to make sure everything stays level as you build, because the framing is unstable until the backerboard goes on. First frame the back and sides by cutting upper channels, then fit the studs between them. Next build the front framing with openings for doors and the barbecue. Make cross braces with tabs and screw the tabs into the upper channel.

❹ Check Openings

Test-fit the doors and cooking units to make sure the openings are the correct sizes. If they are slightly large, cut the backerboard to overhang the framing by up to an inch for a tighter fit. Take into account the thickness of the backerboard, siding material, and countertop when fitting everything together.

❺ Add Backerboard

Measure the ½-inch concrete backerboard for cutting and then subtract ¼ inch, as the edges tend to be ragged. To cut, guide with a straightedge and score one side several times with a utility knife, then snap the piece and score the opposite side. Use a reciprocating saw or jigsaw equipped with a masonry blade for cutouts. Check the framing once more for square, then attach backerboard with concrete backerboard screws every 4 inches or so into the studs and channels. Check once more that the doors and cooking units will fit. Then add backerboard to the top of the counter.

building a wooden counter

Like a metal-framed counter, a wood-framed counter is light enough to rest on a paver patio or deck as long as you don't top it with a heavy concrete countertop. For it to be fire resistant, the wood must be covered with concrete backerboard, but you should also make sure the cooking units have insulating jackets so they aren't hot where they touch the counter. Use pressure-treated lumber, and if you're in a very wet climate, use a piece of composite decking for the bottom plate.

WHAT YOU'LL NEED

2 x 4 or 2 x 3 pressure-treated studs

Composite decking (optional)

Power miter box or radial-arm saw

½" concrete backerboard

2" and 3" deck screws

Drill

Level

Framing square

¾" pressure-treated plywood

2" backerboard screws

❶ Build the Front Wall

Draw out your design and plan the openings so that the grill and doors will fit. The opening for the grill will be covered with ½-inch concrete backerboard, so the wood-framed opening must be 1 inch wider and ½ inch deeper than the finished opening. Make sure there's enough clearance for kitchen door flanges. Cut the bottom plate to the length of the counter minus 1 inch for the backerboard thickness on each end. Then cut the top plate and studs that will fit between them. Assemble on a flat surface, use a framing square to check the corners, then drive two 3-inch deck screws into each joint.

❷ Assemble Four Sides

Build sidewalls and the rear wall in the same manner as the front wall. Working with a helper, hold two walls in position, check the corners for square and make sure the tops are flush. Then connect the sections by driving deck screws into each corner.

❸ Add Top Braces

Cut braces to connect the front and back walls. Position two braces on each side of the sink, if you will have one, and space the others no more than 16 inches apart. Hold a brace flush with the top plate, drill an angled pilot hole on each side, and then drive 3-inch screws.

❹ Add the Plywood Floor

Cut ¾-inch pressure-treated ply-wood pieces to create the floor. Cut notches where the plywood must fit the studs, then fasten down the floor by driving 2-inch deck screws every 8 inches or so.

❺ Cover with Backerboard

See step 5 on page 115 for instructions on cutting backerboard. Attach it to the sides of the counter with 2-inch backerboard screws. Also apply backerboard to the top. If you're planning a tile countertop, make a firm substrate by spreading a layer of thinset mortar on top of the first backerboard layer and then add a second layer of backerboard.

prefabricated counters

WHAT YOU'LL NEED

Dolly

Level

Shims

Chalk line

Pencil

Construction adhesive

Nuts and bolts provided

Adjustable wrench and socket set

Tape measure

Grinder with diamond blade

Radial saw with diamond blade

Eye and ear protection, if making cuts

Masonry drill

Spray bottle

Mortar

Eldorado stone

Grout bag

Metal striking tool

Rag

Soft-bristled brush

People who are new to building may be hesitant to attempt either concrete block, steel, or wood-framed counters. Eldorado Stone, makers of architectural stone veneer for indoor and outdoor uses, sells prefabricated outdoor counter pieces that you can mix and match to create your own outdoor kitchen without needing to build from scratch. The pieces are made of glass- and fiber-reinforced concrete and can be installed on any solid surface without concrete footings. Each cabinet box is shipped with a scratch coat on the sides ready to receive architectural stone veneer, a floated smooth top, and predrilled bolt holes. They are open on the bottom and sides for gas, electrical, and water connections. Eldorado also offers seating-wall, column, bar-height, and raised-backsplash pieces so you can customize your design. Here's how these prefabricated systems work.

❶ Create Layout

Use a dolly to move the prefabricated counter pieces into place on a smooth patio and establish your layout. Make sure the cabinet surfaces are level and line up with adjacent surfaces. Place shims under the cabinets to make them level, if necessary.

❷ Attach Counter Pieces

Mark the layout on your patio with a chalk line and pencil, then move the end piece so that you can apply a bead of construction adhesive to the facing sides. Push the first two pieces back together and use the nuts and bolts provided with the system to tie the pieces together through predrilled holes. Continue until all the pieces are attached.

❸ Make Appliance Cutouts

Measure each cooking appliance and mark the layout on the countertop. Use a grinder with a diamond blade to make cutouts in the concrete tops of the units to hold the appliances. If the appliance manufacturer requires venting, cut out a vent hole using a circular saw fitted with a diamond blade; attach a vent plate to the hole with construction adhesive.

❹ Attach the Cantilever Pieces

If you are using preformed edges or cantilever pieces, put these components in place, making sure edges are flush with the counter surface. Mark where the predrilled holes meet the counter below and drill holes through the counter. Run a bead of construction adhesive along the edge, place the piece on the counter, and bolt it down.

❺ Install the End Caps

At the end of each counter run, you will need to install an end cap. Run a bead of construction adhesive along the end cap opening and push the cap into place.

❻ Install the Veneer Stone

Spray the area with water before applying mortar to the scratch coat and on the back of each piece of Eldorado stone. Using the design worked out when you place your order and following the manufacturer's installation instructions, press each piece into place.

❼ Grout

Use a grout bag to fill the gaps with mortar. Once the mortar can hold a thumbprint, use a metal striking tool to remove any excess from the joints. As soon as possible, use a wet rag to wipe off any mortar that gets on the stones.

❽ Brush the Joints

Remove excess mortar with a dry, soft-bristled brush. Do not use a wet brush, as the additional water can smear the mortar.

stucco facing

Practice stuccoing on a scrap of concrete backerboard until you perfect your technique.

Stucco is a durable masonry finish and a popular choice for outdoor kitchens when the house is also finished with stucco. There are many stucco textures to choose from. The color can be integrated into the wet mix, or you can prime and paint once the stucco is cured. This project shows how to stucco a block wall. If you want to cover concrete backerboard, first apply wire mesh to the corners (see pages 64–65). Don't worry if your base coat doesn't look great. You'll get the hang of it, and the final coat will look more consistent.

❶ Apply the Base Coat

Coat the counter wall with latex bonding agent. Mix stucco following directions on the bag. Once mixed, it should be firm enough to hold its shape when scooped up with a trowel. Place some stucco on a mason's hawk or piece of plywood. Scoop some up with a straight finishing trowel and spread it upward onto the wall, pressing it into place. Cover one wall with a uniform thickness of ½ inch.

❷ Scarify the Base Coat

Before the stucco starts to harden, comb the surface with a scarifying tool. Make one by driving galvanized nails at 1-inch intervals through a piece of 2 x 2. Produce grooves without raising large crumbs. Once the base coat is hard but not quite dry, spray with a fine mist of water and repeat every few daylight hours over two days to slow down the curing process. The slower stucco cures, the stronger it will be.

❸ Apply the Finish Coat

Mix according to the second-coat instructions on the stucco-mix bag. Add liquid colorant to white stucco mix if you want integral color, or you can prime and paint it once it has cured. Apply it to the wall as before. When you come to an outside corner, hold a piece of 1 x 4 against the adjoining wall and apply stucco up to it.

❹ Create a Texture

Start working on the final texture before the stucco starts to dry. To make a swirled texture as shown, set the blade of a masonry trowel in the stucco and rotate it to create half a circle. Make swirls that overlap each other by roughly the same amount. See the box below for other textures. Keep the stucco damp by spraying periodically as before for several days to slow down the curing. If you decide to paint, wait about six weeks and use a primer first that works for masonry surfaces.

design lesson

>> Finishing stucco is an art, and many textures are possible. For a brushed texture, use a mason's brush in short strokes or swirls. For a spatter texture, dip the bristles of a broom into the wet stucco and shake toward the wall. For a knockdown texture, push a trowel flat onto the stucco and pull up to form a pattern of peaks. Wait about 15 minutes, then run a trowel lightly over the surface to flatten some but not all of the peaks.

stone facing

Randomly shaped stone in earthy tones will look natural in most any landscape.

Use irregular flagstone or stone cut into squares or rectangles. Veneer stones, which are thinner and lighter than standard flagstones designed for flooring, are easier to install on a wall. Man-made veneer stones are lighter still (see pages 118–119). Very thick stones must be stacked one on top of the other as though you were building a stone wall, and they will need to be tied to the wall with corrugated metal strips.

WHAT YOU'LL NEED

Sheet of plywood

Flagstones or
veneer stones

Cold chisel

Hammer

Spray bottle

Type S or N mortar

Straight trowel

Small blocks of wood

Rag or sponge

Mortar bag

Small pointed trowel

Metal striking tool

Soft-bristled brush

① Lay Out the Pattern
Take a sheet of plywood as wide as the counter and place it on the ground next to the counter. Lay out the stones, making cuts as necessary, until you are happy with the pattern and have fairly consistent joint widths.

② Skim-coat the Wall
Mist the concrete block or backerboard wall with water and use a straight trowel to apply a stiff coat of type S or N mortar. Press the mortar onto the wall with a straight trowel and create a ⅛-inch-thick coat. Cover an area approximately 5 feet wide, or as much as you can cover with stone before the mortar begins to harden.

③ Set the First Row
Starting with the bottom row, transfer stones from the plywood to the wall. Press each stone into the mortar. They should feel stuck if you try to pull them off. If they don't, back-butter the stone with additional mortar (see step 4). Use blocks of wood or small rocks to give the stones a bit of support, and avoid moving stones once the mortar has begun to harden.

④ Set the Upper Stones
Continue setting stones up the wall. If a lower stone starts to slide, wait for the mortar to set a bit further before proceeding. Back-butter the stones, if they aren't adhering to the mortar on the wall, by applying additional mortar on the backs before placing them. Wipe off any mortar that gets on the stone facing as soon as possible.

⑤ Fill the Joints
Once the mortar has hardened, use a mortar bag or a small pointed trowel to fill the joints. Overfill all the gaps slightly. Then wait until the mortar is stiff enough to hold a thumbprint before you use a metal striking tool to wipe away excess and create a fairly smooth, consistent depth. Use a dry brush to wipe off mortar from the faces of the stones before it dries.

tile facing

Brick-shaped porcelain tiles in a muted color allow the painted blue door to be the focal point of this counter.

Stone or ceramic tiles are a handsome way to finish a concrete block or concrete backerboard-faced counter. Ask the tile dealer if the tiles you choose are rated for outdoor use in your climate. Larger tiles like the ones shown here will be faster to install, but small tiles in an interesting pattern will give the counter a completely different aesthetic. If you choose a porous stone tile, maintain the surfaces with a coat of acrylic sealant every year or two. Ceramic tiles do not need to be sealed, but it's a good idea to seal the grout lines to prevent problems with dirt and mold.

WHAT YOU'LL NEED

Tiles

Snap cutter or wet saw

Rubber gloves

Paintbrush

Acrylic masonry sealer

Thinset mortar

Bucket

Straight trowel

Square-notched trowel

Plastic spacers

Grout

Laminated grout float

Sponge

Soft-bristled brush

❶ Lay Out and Cut Tiles

Draw or dry-lay the tile layout so that you end up with as many whole tiles as possible. If you don't have bullnose edge tiles, plan to run tiles far enough past the edge to hide the unfinished edge of the adjoining tiles. Ceramic tiles can be cut with a snap cutter (see page 128), but you will need to buy or rent a wet saw to cut stone tiles or make clean cutouts in ceramic tile.

❷ Seal Stone Tiles

Seal porous stone tiles before they are installed so that grout doesn't stain them during the installation process. Wear rubber gloves and use a paintbrush to apply acrylic masonry sealer in an even coat on the face of the tiles. The sides of stone tiles should not need to be coated, but if you're using Saltillo or adobe tiles, then the sides should be sealed as well.

❸ Trowel Thinset

Mix a batch of thinset mortar fortified with liquid latex or powdered polymer. Follow the instructions on the bag and let the mixture sit for 10 minutes or so, then stir again before using. Using a trowel with square notches of the size recommended for your tiles, spread thinset onto the counter. Use the flat side of the trowel to press mortar into the counter, then the notched side to spread to a consistent depth.

❹ Set the Tiles

Using your layout as a guide, press tiles into the thinset mortar. The back of each tile should be at least 80 percent covered by the thinset. If not, back-butter the tiles. Make sure the bottom row is level and at a consistent distance from the top of the counter. Use plastic spacers to maintain consistent grout lines. If tiles start to shift, wait until the thinset hardens on that row before continuing.

❺ Grout

Once the thinset mortar has cured for a day or two, it's safe to remove the plastic spacers. Most will pop out easily; use pliers to pull out any that are difficult. Mix a batch of latex- or polymer-fortified grout according to the directions on the package and apply it to the face of the tiles using a laminated grout float. Run the float in several directions to make sure the joints are filled.

❻ Tool the Joints

Once the grout starts to stiffen but well before it dries, use a damp sponge to wipe excess grout off the joints and off the face of the tile. Push the sponge along the grout joints to end up with a consistent depth while making sure the joints are completely sealed. Use a brush to clean grout out of the grooves if you used a rough-faced stone tile.

tiling a countertop

Shiny tiles are easy to wipe clean, but tend to show watermarks.

WHAT YOU'LL NEED

Tiles

½" concrete backerboard

Backerboard knife

Thinset mortar

Square-notched trowel

Fiberglass mesh reinforcing tape

Straight trowel

Pencil

Chalk line

Strips of plywood

Plastic spacers

Snap cutter or wet saw

Tile nibbling tool

Straightedge

2 x 4

Rubber mallet

Painter's tape

Grout

Laminated grout float

Sponge

Bucket

Cheesecloth

Ceramic, porcelain, and stone tiles are all good choices for outdoor kitchen countertops, though some stone will need to be resealed regularly. Ask your tile dealer for products that will stand up to your climate and that are rated for countertop use. Ceramic tile lines often have accessory pieces such as V-caps and bullnose field tiles to hide the edges of the counter (see step 3). Otherwise, you may have to get creative about finishing the edges and corners. This project shows how to install a concrete backerboard substrate and tile over that, but tile can also be installed over a poured concrete substrate (see pages 130–133).

❶ Set the Backerboard

Use a backerboard knife to cut pieces of ½-inch concrete backerboard. Cut holes for appliances and test for fit. Spread thinset mortar on top of the concrete block walls and set the backerboard in the mortar. Or, if you have a wood- or steel-framed counter, screw the backerboard in. Then cut a second layer of backerboard, spread thinset mortar on the bottom layer, and set the top layer in the mortar.

❷ Seal the Edges

Cut and press strips of fiberglass mesh reinforcing tape to fit over the joints and wrap around the edges. Spread a small amount of thinset mortar over the tape using a trowel or small scraping tool. Use just enough to hold the tape in place, and use the thinset to fill any gaps between backerboard sheets.

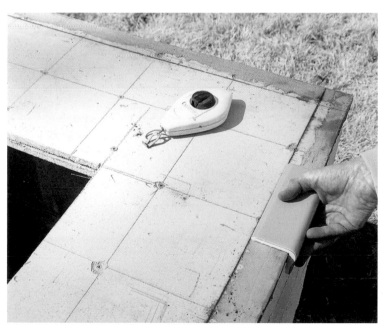

❸ Make Layout Lines

If you are using a ceramic tile V-cap, check to see if it has a raised corner designed to keep water from running off the edge of the countertop. This is helpful indoors, but for an outdoor kitchen you want water to run off. So install the V-cap upside down. In both directions at each corner, hold the V-cap piece in place and trace its edge with a pencil. Snap chalk lines over the trace lines to mark the outside edge of the field tiles.

❹ Dry-Run Tiles

Screw in long, straight pieces of plywood as battens to temporarily mark the outside edges of the field tiles. Lay the field tiles out in a dry run with plastic spacers for grout lines. Adjust the layout as necessary to avoid cuts and narrow tiles as much as possible. Once the layout is complete, make any cuts needed. If you are using porous stone tiles, coat the top of each one with an acrylic sealant before you install them.

continued on page 128

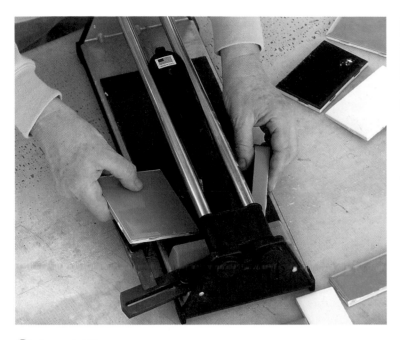

⑤ Cut Tiles

Most ceramic tiles can be cut straight with a snap cutter. Set a tile firmly against the cutter's guide so the cut will be square. Push or pull the cutter all the way across the tile in a single stroke. Place the wings of the cutter on each side of the score line and push down to snap the tile in two. Cutouts that don't need to be precise can be done with a tile nibbling tool; otherwise, use a wet saw.

⑥ Cut Corner Pieces

If using V-caps, you may need to make 45-degree angle cuts at inside or outside corners. For the V-cap's grout lines to line up with those of the field tiles, you also need to cut the V-caps to length. Hold them in place with plastic spacers to mark the cut, and cut with a wet saw.

⑦ Trowel the Thinset

Pick up a section of the dry-laid tiles and set them aside so you can easily replace them in the correct arrangement. Mix a batch of latex- or polymer-reinforced thinset mortar. Spread it onto the backerboard using a square-notched trowel, first with the smooth side and then with the notched side to create an even surface.

⑧ Set the Field Tiles

Begin setting the tiles at a corner where two battens meet. Use plastic spacers to maintain even grout lines as you press each tile into place. Once you have finished with the first 3- to 4-foot-long section, move on to the next one.

9 Maintain Lines and Bed the Tiles

Use a straightedge ruler to check that the edges are straight every few rows. Every so often, pick up a tile and make sure that the mortar covers at least 80 percent of its rear surface. If not, back-butter by applying a thin layer of mortar to the back of the tiles. Also bed each tile by placing a scrap of 2 x 4 over a row and tapping gently over the wood with a rubber mallet.

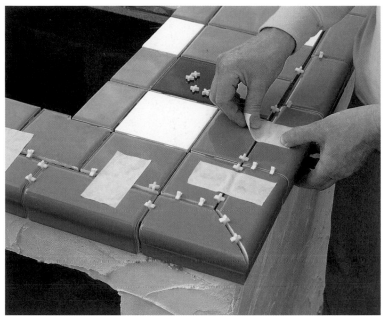

10 Set the V-caps

Once all the field tiles are set, remove the wood battens and set the edge tiles or V-caps if you are using them. First apply mortar to the top and edge of the counter, then put a little in the V-cap as well. Press the V-caps in place and use spacers around each one. Use painter's tape to keep the V-caps in place while the mortar sets.

11 Apply Grout

Once the mortar has fully cured, mix a batch of latex-reinforced grout and apply it to the countertop using a laminated grout float. Press grout into the joints, holding the float nearly flat and moving it in several directions. Then hold the float at an angle to the joints to scrape away the excess mortar without digging into them.

12 Wipe and Tool

Wait until the grout is a bit firmer but not so long that it starts to dry. Using a sponge and a bucket of fresh water, wipe away the excess mortar and press into the joints to create a consistent depth. Keep rinsing the sponge and wiping until all the excess grout is gone and the grout lines are tooled evenly. After the grout has dried, buff the surface with a piece of cheesecloth to remove the grout haze. A week later, seal the grout, or the entire countertop, if you're using stone.

pouring a concrete countertop

Get creative with pattern or color, and be prepared for the concrete to patina over time.

WHAT YOU'LL NEED

½" concrete backerboard

Backerboard knife

Thinset mortar

Square-notched trowel

2 x 4s

2 x 6s

Masonry screws

Nails

Drill

Clamps

Stucco lath

Tin snips

Silicone caulk

High-strength concrete

Concrete colorant, if desired

Fiber reinforcement

Wheelbarrow

Bucket

Rag

Magnesium or Teflon float

Mason's trowel

Hammer

Concrete edger

Plastic wrap

Plastic sheeting

Acrylic masonry sealer or wax

Do-it-yourselfers can attempt simple poured-in-place concrete countertops as finished surfaces or as substrates for tile countertops. They may not be as refined as those produced by professional concrete countertop artists, but they will serve their purpose. If you have experience pouring concrete slabs, you might attempt some decorative elements such as texture or pattern. Or you can grind and polish the top after it has cured for a silky-smooth finish, and experiment with concrete colorants to create something other than gray. Expect a few hairline cracks over time and keep the counter protected by applying an acrylic masonry sealer every year, as concrete is extremely porous.

❶ Build the Form

Install the concrete backerboard substrate (see page 127) and temporarily prop scrap wood underneath for support. Then cut 2 x 4s to wrap around the top of the exterior walls of the counter and prop them up temporarily or screw them into the counter. This will allow the finished countertop to extend 1½ inches over the counter. On the outside of the 2 x 4s, cut pieces of 2 x 6 for the main form; screw them into place.

❷ Add Reinforcing Metal and Seal

Stucco lath works well to reinforce a small concrete countertop. Cut it to fit about an inch from the perimeter of the form and then set it aside. Apply silicone caulk to seal any gaps around the wood form so that liquid concrete will not leak out. At the corners, apply a bead of caulk to help make the finished edges round rather than sharp.

❸ Mix the Concrete

If you're using integral color, experiment with concrete pigments until you achieve a mix you like. Let the sample dry fully and apply masonry sealer to see the true color. Develop a precise recipe so you can be consistent with each batch of concrete mix. Put dry concrete, colorant (if you're using it), and fiber reinforcement to strengthen the mix into a wheelbarrow, add water, and mix to a consistency that is completely wet but not pourable.

❹ Spread the First Layer

Wipe the backerboard with a wet rag so the concrete adheres. Shovel concrete into a bucket, then dump it into the center of the formed area. Starting in the middle and working outward, use a magnesium or Teflon float to spread the concrete so that it's about half the thickness of the countertop. Press down as you spread it to make sure the concrete sticks to the backerboard.

continued on page 132

⑤ Set the Reinforcement

Set the precut reinforcing metal on top of the concrete. Add another layer of concrete on top and spread, pushing down to prevent voids and bubbles. If the wood form bulges while you work, straighten it with bar clamps. Continue spreading until the form is full. Then set a piece of 2 x 4 that spans the form boards and screed the top so that it's level with the tops of the form boards.

⑥ Eliminate Bubbles

Air bubbles often occur where the concrete meets the form. To minimize this, slip a mason's trowel down between the boards and the concrete and move it along the perimeter using a slicing motion. Then tap the sides of the form with a hammer.

⑦ Float the Concrete

As soon as any bleed water on top of the concrete disappears, run a magnesium or Teflon float across the surface to begin smoothing. Press just hard enough to bring up a little bleed water, then stop floating. The reason you want to avoid floating when bleed water is present is that it makes the final surface weak and prone to flaking.

⑧ Use an Edger

Run a concrete edger along the perimeter two or three times until the surface is smooth, but only when bleed water is not present. As soon as the water disappears, run a magnesium or Teflon float over the surface to smooth the resulting ridge.

⑨ Strip the Form

Once the concrete is hard enough to hold its shape, carefully release the squeeze clamps. If the form bulges, tighten the clamps, wait 10 minutes or so, and try again. Once all the clamps are off, unscrew the form boards and slowly pull them away.

⑩ Smooth the Edge

If you like the way the edge looks, leave it alone. Otherwise, smooth it with a magnesium float and then a steel trowel. If any bubbles are visible, fill them by hand with more concrete and then trowel again.

⑪ Smooth the Corners

Use a float or trowel to roughly achieve a rounded edge if you desire. Then use a piece of plastic wrap to finish rounding and smoothing.

⑫ Finish the Surface

Go over the surface once more with a steel trowel, but avoid overworking. If troweling begins to roughen rather than smooth the surface, it's time to stop. Cover the countertop with plastic to keep the concrete wet so it can cure slowly over a few days. Once it has fully cured, in about 30 days, apply two coats of acrylic masonry sealer or wax. Reapply sealer yearly or wax monthly to avoid stains.

gas and propane hookups

PROPANE CONNECTIONS
Always have an extra tank on hand.

Consult your grill's owner's manual before you begin. A typical connection includes a regulator, which ensures that the grill will receive the right amount of propane, as well as a fitting and rubber hose. If you have two propane cooking units, purchase a setup like the one shown in the illustration below. Most fittings are designed to be connected by hand; do not use pliers or other tools, and make the connections with care. The fitting's nipple should be centered in the hole in the tank's valve, then hold the fitting straight as you screw it in. If you encounter resistance, stop and try again or you may cause leaks.

CHECKING FOR PROPANE LEAKS
Test for leaks whenever you hook up a tank.

Purchase a special gas-testing fluid, or mix a solution of one part water to one part dishwashing soap. Open the tank's valve and spread the fluid or soapy water on the areas shown below. If you see growing bubbles where the fitting meets the tank's valve, shut off the valve and try retightening the fitting. If you see growing bubbles on the tank itself, call your propane gas supplier or the fire department.

Hookup for a Multiburner Grill Plus a Side Burner

Side burner valve

Rubber hose

Regulator

Multiple burner control valves

Where to Test for Leaks

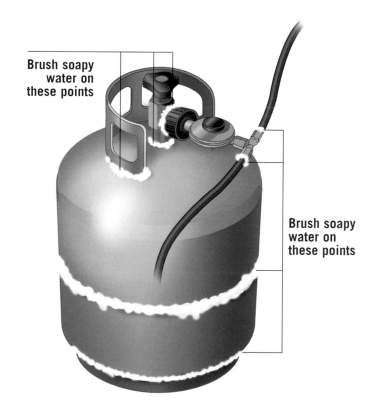

Brush soapy water on these points

Brush soapy water on these points

NATURAL-GAS CONNECTIONS
A professional who knows local codes should make hookups for you.

The contractor will make sure the gas is shut off at the meter. Codes may require a separate shutoff for each gas unit. A length of pipe extending downward a foot or so, called a drip leg, is often required at each valve. Two valves with drip legs require a variety of fittings as shown in the illustration below. With solid steel gas pipe, the male threads will be wrapped with yellow Teflon tape made for gas pipe before the connections are made. A regulator, which usually comes with the grill, will be installed in the line between the shutoff valve and the grill.

CHECKING FOR GAS LEAKS
Do not skip this critical step.

When all connections are secure, make sure the grill and burners are off, then turn the gas back on. Use the soapy-water test described on page 134. Also turn off all gas appliances in the house and check your gas meter. If it shows any sign of movement after five minutes or so, call your plumber back to look for the problem.

Dual Gas Valves

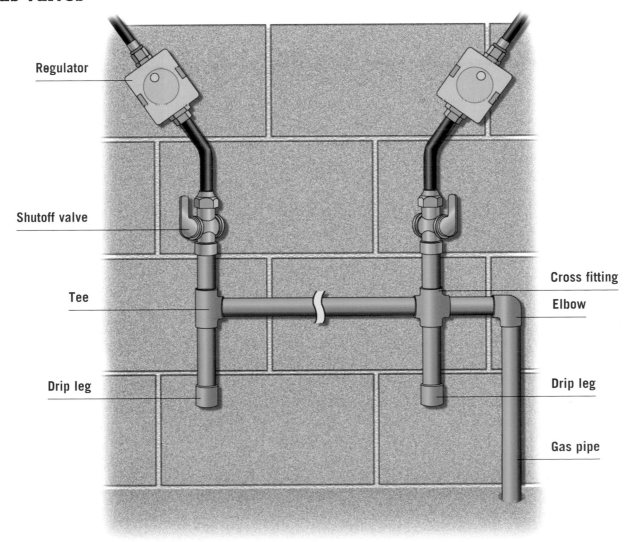

Regulator

Shutoff valve

Tee

Drip leg

Cross fitting

Elbow

Drip leg

Gas pipe

electrical connections

Choose fixtures that enhance the style and function of your outdoor kitchen.

Hire an electrician to run the electrical line to your outdoor kitchen and to make sure that the appliances you plan to use will not overload the circuit. Once you have a single conduit inside the counter, you can install a number of receptacles or light fixtures. Some of the most common connections are shown here. Be absolutely certain the main power is off at the circuit panel before undertaking any wiring projects.

HOOK UP A GFCI RECEPTACLE   Hire an electrician if you have any doubts.

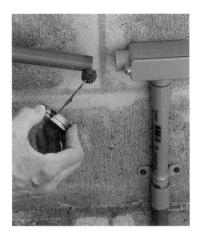

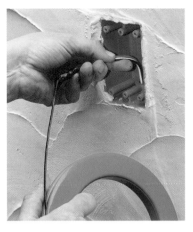

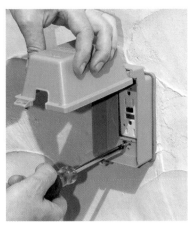

① Install Branch Lines

Check with your local building department to see if you can use PVC conduit to run exposed outdoor wiring or if you are required to use metal conduit. Cut all the pipes to the desired lengths and assemble the pipes and fittings in a complete dry run. Then draw layout lines on the fittings and pipes to indicate how they should fit together. Then disassemble the pieces, keeping them in order. Working in order, apply PVC cement to the inside of the fitting and the end of the pipe (some regions require primer before the cement), then immediately insert the pipe into the fitting, twist slightly, and hold for 15 seconds.

② Pull Wires

Once the conduit is glued together and anchored to the walls every 16 inches using pipe straps and masonry screws, pull wires through the conduit. Use a fish tape or a pulling fitting to push them to the other side. Wrap the wires (usually there are three: a black hot wire, a white neutral wire, and a bare ground wire) around the end of the fish tape and secure them with electrical tape. Turn the fish tape's crank to reel the wires back through the conduit.

③ Connect a Receptacle

Ground-fault circuit interrupter receptacles (GFCIs) are generally required for outdoor installations. First turn power off at the main circuit panel, then double-check the wires with a circuit tester. Remove about 1 inch of insulation from the ends of the black and white wires with wire strippers. Bend exposed wire ends in a loop and hook the black wire around the brass terminal screw marked LINE, then tighten the screw. Connect the white wire the same way to the silver screw marked LINE. Then hook the ground wire to the green terminal and tighten the screw. If you want to run power from this receptacle to others, hook those wires to the terminals marked LOAD. All extensions of the first GFCI receptacle in the line will also be GFCI-protected.

④ Add an In-use Cover

If the receptacle is exposed, install an in-use cover that protects it from rain even when appliances are plugged into it. Install the gaskets carefully so the cover will be watertight.

construction lesson

》 Low-voltage landscape lighting can be easily installed in or around your outdoor kitchen. Buy a kit and enough low-voltage cord to reach your destination. Attach the transformer to a wall near a GFCI receptacle, run the cord in a shallow trench to the counter, and anchor the light.

A farmhouse sink adds considerable style and function to this stone-faced kitchen. Follow the installation instructions for the specific model you buy.

It's best to have a professional plumber run supply and drain lines before you pour the concrete slab, but you may choose to hook up the sink and faucet yourself. The instructions that follow will give you a general idea of the process. If at any time you are unsure of the procedure while attempting this job, stop and phone a professional to get it done right.

SUNSET CONTRIBUTING EDITOR
PETER O. WHITELEY

on tankless water heaters

>> Enjoy instant hot water in your outdoor kitchen without running a separate hot-water line by installing a small electric on-demand heater fitted to the cold water pipe under your counter. This appliance is easy to install; simply mount it inside the counter, hook up the pipes, and plug it into a 120-volt receptacle equipped with a GFCI (see illustration).

Under-counter Plumbing Hookups

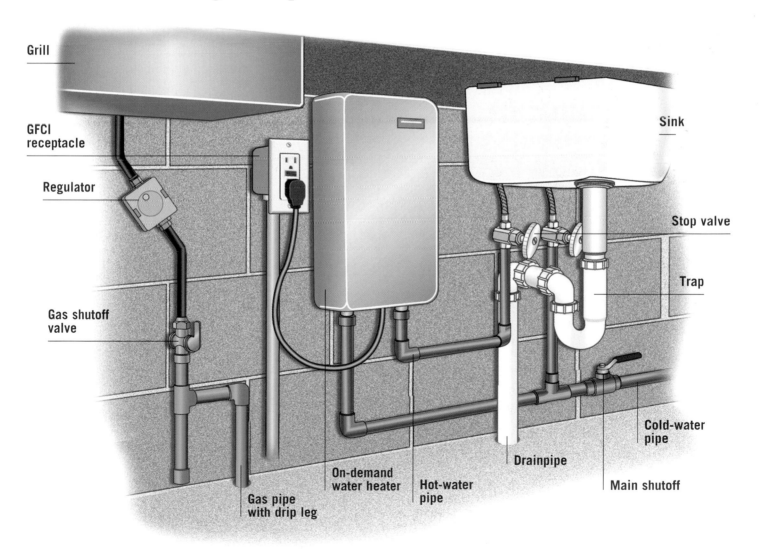

Grill

GFCI receptacle

Regulator

Gas shutoff valve

Gas pipe with drip leg

On-demand water heater

Hot-water pipe

Drainpipe

Main shutoff

Cold-water pipe

Trap

Stop valve

Sink

continued on page 140

INSTALLING THE SINK AND FAUCET   Work carefully and test for leaks.

❶ Install Stop Valves

Plumbing codes call for stop valves so that you can quickly turn off water to a faucet in an emergency. Buy stop valves that fit the size of the water supply pipes and tubes leading to the faucet. If you have copper supply pipes, you'll need to solder the joints. Hire a professional if you are not comfortable working with copper pipes.

❷ Install a Basket Strainer

Turn the sink upside down on a pair of workhorses. Disassemble a basket strainer and apply plumber's putty to the flange. From underneath, press the strainer into place and hold it firmly with the handles of a pair of pliers. From above, slip on the rubber washer, the cardboard washer, and the hold-down nut. Tighten the nut using large slip-joint pliers.

❸ Assemble the Trap

If codes allow, use a plastic trap and tighten the nuts with slip-joint pliers. Install the correct washers at each joint. For a single-bowl sink, install a tailpiece onto the strainer, then add the trap piece. Set the sink in place temporarily to see if you need to cut the tailpiece to line it up with the drainpipe. Set the sink back on the horses and tighten the joints.

❹ Install the Faucet

Single-handle faucets are typically installed with copper inlet tubes running through the center hole. Double-handle faucets typically have inlets that run through both of the mounting holes, as shown. Follow the manufacturer's instructions for anchoring the faucet to the sink. Attach braided supply tubes to the inlets and tighten firmly. Set the sink in place and check for fit.

⑤ Set the Sink

Once you are sure everything will fit, press a rope of plumber's putty to the underside of the sink's flange. If you have a stainless-steel sink, slide two or more mounting clips onto each side of the flange and use plumber's putty to hold the clips still while you set the sink. Lower the sink into place, check the seal, and press down. Cast-iron sinks will not require clips.

⑥ Tighten the Mounting Clips

From under the sink, position the clips so that they grab the counter. Tighten the clips using a screwdriver. From above, check that the sink is sealed all the way around. Putty should ooze out of the flange at every point. Once the clips are tightened, clean away excess putty.

⑦ Connect the Supply Lines

Attach supply tubes to the stop valves. Hot goes to the left handle and cold to the right handle. Tighten each nut using two wrenches as shown so that you don't kink the faucet's copper tubes as you tighten. Turn off the faucet and turn on the water supply, then check for leaks. Tighten further as needed.

⑧ Connect the Drain Line

Slide on nuts and washers and tighten the nuts to connect the drain line. To test the drain for leaks, plug the sink, fill it with water, then pull the plug. Use a flashlight to look for leaks. If the pipes are not dry, tighten the nuts again. The S-trap arrangement shown is an example only; check local codes for the required drain configuration.

install grills and doors

Find stainless-steel doors at outdoor-living stores or online.

Once the counter and countertop are complete and the hookups are ready, it's time to install the grill and cabinet doors. You want to avoid having rainwater seep through gaps around either the grill or the doors. The best way to keep the inside of the counter dry is to cover it during the rainy season, but you should also put a bead of high-quality silicone caulk around the edges. Aim for one smooth bead that seals completely; if it doesn't, scrape it away and try again rather than apply a second bead on top.

INSTALLING A GRILL OR COOKTOP Thoroughly read the instructions that came with your model.

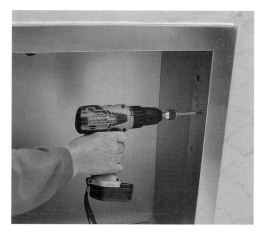

❶ Set in Place

Measure to see that the gas line will reach the shutoff valve if you're installing a gas grill, then carefully lift the grill into place and have a second person thread the gas line through the opening as you go. Hook it up to the gas line or propane tank, turn it on, and test for leaks (see pages 134–135).

❷ Caulk Around the Grill

Fill any gaps larger than ¼ inch between the grill and countertop with latex-fortified grout, then wait for it to dry before applying caulk. For grills with removable or adjustable flanges, first apply one bead of caulk to seal the gap between the grill and the countertop. Once the caulk is dry, apply a second bead under or around the flange. Otherwise, caulk the area around the opening and set the grill on top of the caulk. Apply caulk to the front face of the grill as well.

❸ Seal the Flange

If possible, apply a bead of caulk under the flange, then lower the flange onto the wet caulk. Also apply caulk where the flange meets the grill and wipe excess away while it is still wet.

INSTALLING A DOOR Dry-fit all doors before mounting.

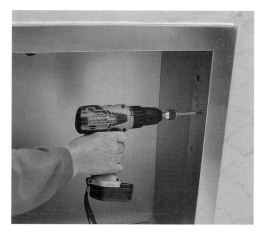

❶ Prepare the Opening

If the door is too tight when you dry-fit it in the hole, try scraping away excess mortar or grout to clear enough room. Hold the door in position, flat against the counter's wall, and drill pilot holes for the screws into a solid surface such as concrete block or stone facing. Remove the door, wipe away dust, and apply a generous bead of caulk to the door's flange.

❷ Install the Door

Press the door into place, making sure the caulk seals the flange at all points. Drive masonry screws into the pilot holes if yours is a concrete block counter. Otherwise use sheet-metal screws for steel framing or wood screws for wood framing.

Finishing the Look

As with indoor kitchens, planning for an outdoor kitchen involves a long list of choices and multiple shopping expeditions. To create a cohesive design, you need to consider how the facing material for the counter, the countertop, the patio or deck surface, and surrounding walls will work together. Plan for overhead structures and ways to keep the dining area cool and comfortable all season long, and think about what types of plants will make the outdoor living space blend with the landscape. This chapter provides advice on shopping for grills and appliances, plus all the amenities you may desire to make your outdoor kitchen as functional as the one inside your house.

Chocolate Heath Ceramics tile wraps around the sides and top of this outdoor counter, while a lighter shade visually connects the adjacent low wall and the open storage space under the counter.

siding and
countertops

Outdoor kitchen counters are usually constructed of concrete block, wood studs, or steel studs. The substructure is then faced with a finish material of your choice, such as stone or stucco. You may opt to face the counter with the same material used as siding on your house, match it to the surrounding patio, or select a new material. The only requirement is that the material you choose will stand up to normal weather conditions in your area. Countertop materials should also be weather resistant, especially if they are not protected by an overhead structure. The following pages show options for siding and countertops.

Natural Stone

Thin cut stones suitable for vertical installations are often referred to as flagstone, veneer stone, or face stone. When working with randomly sized stone, lay out the pattern on the ground before installing the pieces on the counter to make sure you can fill all the voids.

Faux Stone

Faux stone veneer, cast from molds of natural stone, can look identical to the real thing. The lighter weight makes it easier to install for do-it-yourselfers. It costs about half what natural stone does, and it allows you to use sizes and shapes that would be difficult to install if they were natural stones.

Ceramic Tiles

There are almost too many choices in ceramic tile, but you can limit them somewhat by determining which options will survive in your climate. Some cannot withstand freezing temperatures. Create a colorful pattern with a mix of glazed ceramics, or choose large porcelain or terra-cotta tiles to cover the area uniformly. Ask the tile dealer if there are preformed pieces for outside corners and the edge of the countertop in the style you choose. A contrasting grout color will make each tile pop, while grout matched to the tiles will allow the pieces to visually blend together. Be sure to seal the grout once it's cured to prevent mold and stains.

Stone Tiles

While face stone is purchased at landscape supply yards, cut stone tiles are generally found at tile and home stores because they are the same as what you would install indoors. Polished stone has a more refined look but may show water marks more than honed or irregular surface textures.

Brick

Outdoor kitchen counters faced with brick are generally also built from the ground up with the same material, but you can also face a concrete-block counter with a single row of brick or apply a thin layer of brick veneer. Brick comes in a variety of colors.

Stucco

For uniform color, stucco is the go-to choice. Applied over concrete block or brick, stucco takes a fair amount of time to install because it requires two or three coats and curing time. Hire an experienced installer, or practice on a separate surface until you have perfected the texture you're going for.

Wood

Wooden counters will do much better under a solid overhang or patio roof if you live in a wet climate. Whether you stain the wood, paint it, or keep it natural, protect it with one or two coats of acrylic sealant annually to prevent water damage and rotting.

Stone or Composite Slab

The most popular choice for indoor kitchens is also appropriate for outside, though some options are lower maintenance than others. Most varieties of granite will need only occasional resealing outdoors, and there are composite slabs made of concrete, resin, and quartz or glass that require minimal maintenance. Marble, limestone, and soft stones will stain and scratch more easily than granite. Slab material will need to be fabricated off-site by a professional and then installed, so factor that cost in with the price of the material. Generally a substrate is not needed for slab countertops unless your design calls for an overhang for bar seating.

Tile

Glazed ceramic tile is easy to wipe clean, and most lines include accessories such as preformed cap, end, and bullnose pieces, making it easy to create a finished look. If you drop something very heavy on ceramic tile, it may crack. Otherwise, as long as you choose tiles rated for the climate in which you live, they will survive nicely outdoors. Some types of stone tile, such as slate and honed granite, work well as countertops, but others may not be strong enough for countertop use. If the stone you choose is porous, apply several coats of acrylic sealant. Tile requires a substrate of concrete or concrete backerboard (see pages 126–133).

Concrete

The chameleon of countertop materials, concrete can be shaped, formed, and colored to give it many different looks. For outdoor kitchens, concrete countertops are typically poured in place, but there are also artisans who create preformed concrete countertops off-site. Fiber cement countertops look like concrete but are lighter and less prone to surface cracks. All concrete is porous unless treated with sealant. When water no longer beads on the surface, it's time for a new coat. Wax also protects concrete from water, and it creates a beautiful patina over time.

Brick and Flagstone

If you want the outdoor kitchen to blend in with the surrounding hardscape, a brick or rough stone counter will give it a more rustic look. The surface will be uneven, but if you aren't doing a lot of food prep there, then it might not matter. Coat the stone or brick with an acrylic sealant so that spills and dirt are easier to wipe off. Use a stiff-bristled brush to clean around the edges. Avoid varieties of stone that tend to chip off in large chunks, such as sandstone.

Plywood cabinets
with maple doors
don't require a
concrete slab.

C heck with your local building department to be
sure an existing concrete slab is strong enough
to support the heft of your proposed outdoor
kitchen. Concrete-block counters, particularly those with
poured concrete inside the block cells, generally require
a 12-inch concrete footing. If you decide to pour a new

concrete slab instead of smaller footings for the counter,
there are several finishing options (see next page). Outdoor kitchens on wooden decks can work as long as you
build the counter structure with lighter wood or steel
framing rather than concrete block.

PATIO AND DECK MATERIALS Match the finish to the counter or other hardscaping in the garden.

Stone

Cover a concrete slab with random or precision-cut flagstone for a textural, slip-resistant surface. Options include granite, limestone, sandstone, slate, and bluestone. Select a stone quarried close to where you live for environmental and cost reasons, and limit yourself to two types of stone in the garden for a more cohesive and natural feel.

Wood

Steel-framed counters or wooden cabinets are light enough to sit directly on a deck. Look for eco-friendly choices such as reclaimed or Forest Stewardship Council-certified woods, and composite decking made of recycled plastic and sawdust.

Concrete

A concrete patio doesn't have to be smooth and gray. Apply a stain to the final layer, stamp the surface to give it texture and pattern, inset rows of stone or brick to break up the expanse, or add aggregate stones on top. Concrete patios can also be paved with cut stone, brick, or tile.

Brick

Mortar bricks onto a concrete slab or dry-lay them on level soil with sand. Bricks are available in many colors, and salvaged bricks offer rustic designs. Clean any moss that grows in the low spots that accumulate water, or it may become a hazard. Buy SX-rated bricks if you live in an area where the ground freezes and thaws.

design lesson

» A poured concrete slab can be made very smooth or given a rough brushed or aggregate surface. Think about how the surface will be used before deciding on the finish texture. If there's a pool nearby and children at play, some amount of texture is advisable for slip resistance. Too much texture, however, will make heavy dining chairs hard to move around. Stone and brick can also be found in varying levels of smoothness, but the mortar or soil between them makes the overall surface less slippery.

walls

Ceramic tiles on a high wall make this outdoor kitchen look like an indoor one.

Low garden walls give some shelter from breezes, provide extra seating, and create the illusion of an outdoor room. Face the walls with the same material as your patio, or match the outdoor kitchen counter. Higher walls can block noise from nearby roads or neighboring homes, especially if you add the sounds of a fountain. They also create a secluded space for outdoor dinner parties, making you feel as though you're worlds away from home.

WALL FUNCTIONS   Make your walls serve double duty.

Room Divider

Low walls create more intimate spaces in large backyards. Think of them as indoor walls, leading guests from one space to the next. Make sure the top is flat enough to serve as extra seating.

View Blocker

High walls are sometimes necessary to hide unsightly views. A framed mirror breaks up the expanse of corrugated metal and bounces light back into the dining area.

Wind Catcher

Where persistent winds are a problem, high walls aren't always the best solution. Consider a lattice wall, dense plantings, or a wall with random openings to diffuse the wind throughout a large area. Slatted walls like the one shown above slow down wind while still allowing some air circulation.

Noise Reducer

A fountain on a wall adds movement and reflection and muffles the sounds of traffic and neighbors. Depending on the amount of noise you're dealing with, you may get by with the soft trickle of a wall-mounted fountain, or you may need the steady stream of a waterfall like the one shown above.

overhead structures

Halogen lights are hardwired into this wooden overhead.

The chef and guests gathered around the grill will appreciate a little shade. If you're going to have an overhead structure, plan to build it while the outdoor kitchen is being constructed so that posts can be integrated into the design. Be sure the structure is far enough away from the flames so as not to pose a fire hazard. Structures such as patio roofs and gazebos generally require building permits to ensure that such safety considerations are observed, and your neighborhood may have height and placement restrictions. Check with your local building department during the planning stages to avoid any surprises or unhappy neighbors.

BUILT-IN OPTIONS Let in as much or as little sun as you desire.

Complete Protection

A solid-roofed structure, either freestanding or extending out from the house, provides shelter from sun and inclement weather and allows you to cook outdoors for a greater part of the year. Consider adding a ceiling fan approved for outdoor use to increase airflow so that cooking smoke doesn't stagnate.

Sun Diffuser

This louvered patio roof is high enough that cooking flames cannot reach it. Wooden slats spaced an inch apart reduce midday sun without blocking the light altogether.

Shade Maker

Arbors and pergolas consist of posts supporting an open roof of beams or lattice. They provide some shade on their own, or you can have plants grow across them for additional protection. Such overhead structures also visually separate the outdoor kitchen space from the rest of the garden.

outdoor furniture

Powder-coated metal furniture withsands the elements and is easy to keep clean.

W hen shopping for outdoor furniture, look for solid, well-constructed pieces that will last. Poorly made furniture or pieces not designed for outdoor use will soon need to be replaced, negating any initial savings. Look for furniture made from sustainably harvested wood and constructed with mortise-and-tenon joinery. Marine-quality hardware and finishes protect furniture from rust and water damage. Some wooden furniture ages gracefully with no maintenance, while other types need a yearly coat of penetrating oil to protect them from sun and water.

DINING OPTIONS Choose furniture that adds style to your outdoor kitchen.

Tables

Particularly if you plan to use your outdoor kitchen for entertaining, buy a table that can seat eight people. In areas without shade, an umbrella in the center of the table makes midday meals more comfortable in summer. When the table will be exposed to the elements, the top should have slats like the one shown above so that water doesn't pool on the surface.

Seating

Dining chairs should be comfortable for long, leisurely meals. Buy cushions for wooden chairs and store them indoors during the off-season so they stay clean and dry. Lightweight chairs made of woven plant fiber or aluminum are easier to slide in and out on uneven patio surfaces than heavy wooden chairs. There are also woven plastic chairs made with recycled materials that resist wear and fading.

Mix and Match

Well-made, sustainable-wood furniture can be expensive. Another option is to buy second-hand sets, or mix and match used tables and chairs from various sources. For example, the wooden farmhouse table with turned legs shown above is paired with Shaker-style benches. The painted rattan chairs have a Moroccan feel, yet the trio of styles works beautifully outdoors.

design lesson

>> In addition to Forest Stewardship Council-certified and recycled-wood furniture options, there are sustainable and long-lasting grasses such as woven seagrass, water hyacinth, and abaca that make comfortable chairs. Finish wooden furniture with no-VOC stains and sealants or natural penetrating oils that contain no toxic chemicals.

plants

Framed by trees and flowering plants, this kitchen blends seamlessly into the backyard.

Once you've built an outdoor kitchen and outfitted the space for patio dining, it's time to think about some plantings. If you've situated your outdoor kitchen within an existing garden, it may already be surrounded by trees and shrubs and may need little more than a few well-positioned containers or spillers and fillers tucked into surrounding stone walls. In new landscapes, select plants that thrive in your region and do well with the amount of sun they will receive at your site.

GREENERY WITH A PURPOSE   Use plants for style and function.

Enveloping

Leafy foliage surrounding the dining area can make you forget that you're still at home. It's easier to excavate an area among existing, mature plants to achieve this feeling, though it can be done with tall potted plants and fast-growing hedges as well.

Style Setting

The types of plants you choose can introduce a theme or support color palettes and furniture choices meant to evoke a mood or place. Above, a wall of tropical plants and potted succulents sets the mood for an Asian-inspired low table and floor cushions.

Layering

Provide shade, block unwanted views, add color and texture, and make the outdoor kitchen blend with the rest of the garden by layering plants. On the patio above, there are large trees surrounding the dining area, climbing vines providing shade and softening the house, containers adding seasonal color, and hedges that act as outdoor walls.

Blocking

Sit at the dining table and notice what meets your gaze as you look around the garden. Is there an unsightly shed or a view into your neighbor's yard? Hedges of evergreen shrubs or clumping trees can solve such problems. Boxwood, bottlebrush, hop bush, and juniper are good options for natural screens.

creating shade

Create a temporary canopy using heavy pots, bamboo stalks, and a piece of leftover fabric.

Beyond the standard patio umbrella, there are a number of ways to keep people out of the sun while they are cooking or dining. Make sure that whatever covering you choose is kept a safe distance from the grill.

SUN PROTECTION With one of these solutions, you'll be made in the shade.

Cabanas

Cabanas are more typical of tropical poolside vacation resorts, but their solid roofs can be put to good use over outdoor dining areas as well. Leave the fabric walls tied up on each side to let in the cool breeze, or close them to block the glare.

Fabric

Billowy fabric draped across taut wires creates a tropical mood. Fabric made to withstand the elements is usually stiffer than what is shown here. When using sheer fabric, be prepared to take it down and clean it every couple of weeks. Shade sails are a more modern, angular application of this concept.

Umbrellas

They come in a variety of sizes and colors and collapse conveniently when not needed. A movable base filled with sand will support free-standing models. When the umbrella will be used only for dining, it's more convenient to install it in the center of the table. Make sure the reach extends to both sides.

Modern Minimalism

When an overhead doesn't work with the aesthetic of your backyard design but shade is still required, consider running taut wires over the top of the outdoor kitchen and growing a climbing vine. It may take a couple of seasons, but eventually the vine will provide enough shade on its own and look luxurious.

Side-Arm Umbrella

A swing-arm base allows an umbrella to provide shade without becoming a tripping hazard. These side-arm umbrellas are a great solution when space is tight or the traffic pattern would be interrupted by an umbrella with a center support.

SUNSET MARKET EDITOR
JESS CHAMBERLAIN ON

shade versus sun protection

» Creating a shady place to cook and eat keeps you cool, but it may not provide UV protection from the sun's rays. When constructing a cabana, shade sail, or pergola cover, choose fabrics that have tight construction and allow very little sunlight through. Dark colors block more harmful UV rays than light colors. Also look for outdoor fabric that won't fade over time, resists mold and mildew, and can be cleaned with soap and water.

Flexible Sun Coverage

Retractable awnings provide sun and rain protection when you need it and can disappear with the flip of a switch. Choose a well-respected brand that comes with a warranty to make sure the mechanisms and fabric will last for years to come.

Complete Protection

In cold or humid climates, outdoor kitchens are often constructed against the house with three solid or screened walls and a solid roof. Venting the grill becomes more important in such partially enclosed settings, but it can be done. This type of structure will still make you feel more like you're eating outdoors because of the added light and fresh air coming through the screened windows. And you will be able to enjoy it year-round without worrying about mosquitoes, rain, and strong winds.

staying comfortable

This covered patio features built-in infrared heaters for winter and ceiling fans to move the air during summer.

I t's not 80 degrees and sunny every day, which is why there are several man-made options for warming or cooling outdoor living spaces. Depending on where you live, space heaters or misters may be the way to extend your outdoor dining season. Flyng pests, such as wasps and mosquitoes, are another problem that tends to come up with the seasons. Help is available for these sorts of nuisances as well.

In milder climates, a single portable heat lamp may be all you need to make the space comfortable as the sun goes down.

Space Heaters

Portable, propane-powered heaters have an effective range of about 15 to 25 feet and are safer to use than fireplaces or fire pits when young children or pets are a factor. A more elaborate solution is an infrared heater hardwired to an appropriately sized electrical system or plugged into an outdoor-rated receptacle. These heaters warm objects and people rather than surrounding air, and because of the intense heat they emit, they must be installed at least 8 feet above the ground. Hanging above the dining area in evenly spaced rows, they are out of the way and heat the space effectively.

Misters

There are several options for outdoor misters that generate a fine spray of water to make you feel refreshed without getting drenched. Some are fans that shoot mist out, while others are pump and hose systems that can be attached to overhead structures like arbors or the underside of an umbrella. These are best used away from the dining area so that food and place settings do not get wet.

Bees and Yellow Jackets

Bees are generally not out to attack and will not linger if you don't have plants they love on the table. But yellow jackets will go after meat and sweet liquids. Make sure you don't leave food out or rotting fruit around the garden to attract them. If small nests do form, choose a nontoxic, animal- and plant-safe product to spray each nest with at dawn or dusk when there is little activity in the hive. Then wait a couple of days before removing the nest with a stick. Professionals should handle large nests for safety reasons.

Mosquitoes

Citronella candles and incense sticks will deter mosquitoes but may not be appetizing scents. In some areas of the country, mosquitoes are a major problem and people generally choose to eat in screened rooms or porches. People who live in areas with few mosquitoes can avoid larger problems by making sure there is no standing water in the garden where eggs can hatch.

appliances

A complete outdoor kitchen with a large grill and side burners makes cooking for a crowd more enjoyable.

A stand-alone gas grill or charcoal barbecue can suffice for occasional outdoor cooking. In some backyards there isn't space for much more than this, and there are models that come with handy fold-down extensions on the sides to hold plates and utensils.

When you begin to crave additional cooking space and amenities, however, a counter with a drop-in grill, such as the ones described in Chapter 2 of this book, is a better option than a counter rigged up around a stand-alone grill.

GRILL OPTIONS Choose the heat source that provides the flavor you're looking for.

Gas Grills

Powered by liquid propane, which comes in tanks, or by the natural-gas line that runs to your home. Models are generally not interchangeable, so determine the preferred gas source before you buy. Fans of gas grills love that they're ready to use right away; they're also easy to clean and don't impart a charcoal flavor.

Shopping Tips for Gas Grills
» First check to see if you can tap into the main gas line at your house.
» When that's not possible, buy a propane-powered model.
» Painted steel frames can rust, so look for high-quality stainless-steel or cast-aluminum parts.
» Take a magnet when you shop for a grill. It will stick to cheaper grades of stainless steel; choose 300-series stainless.
» Stainless-steel and cast-iron grates are sturdy and resist rust, while unfinished cast iron must be seasoned regularly to prevent rusting.
» Look for a removable bottom and a grate that catches and vaporizes drippings.

Charcoal Grills

Traditionally a stand-alone appliance, but you can find drop-in units for outdoor counters. Charcoal enthusiasts don't mind waiting for the coals to heat up, or the somewhat messy cleanup. They're hooked on the way charcoal makes the food taste.

Shopping Tips for Charcoal Grills
» Look for models made of powder-coated, porcelain-enameled, or high-quality stainless steel.
» A crank that lowers and raises the cooking grate will give you more control.
» Make sure the ash pan is easy to use.

Electric Grills

Don't negatively affect air quality the way wood and charcoal grills do. These units can be portable or built in. Depending on the size, you may need only a 110-volt receptacle rated for outdoor use or 220 volts and a dedicated circuit.

Infrared Grills

Direct intense heat at the food to cook it quickly, locking in moisture and flavor. These appliances can be fueled by natural gas, electricity, or propane and can be purchased as stand-alone units or attached to a grill.

Smokers

Separate the food from the heat source and include a water pan, resulting in smoky flavor and moist meat. They can be found as vertical and horizontal (off-set) models. Charcoal is often the preferred method with smokers, but you can find electric and gas models as well.

SUNSET FOOD EDITOR
MARGO TRUE ON

whole-animal cooking

In many cultures, roasting a whole animal is nothing new. But for many people in North America, it's a fascinating (and increasingly trendy) way to learn about meat and eat it with less waste. By far the easiest approach to cooking a whole animal is in a portable Caja China, a Cuban-style roasting box. Made of plywood and lined with aluminum, it has wheels at one end and two sturdy handles at the other. A drip pan rests on the bottom of the box, and the animal (butterflied by your butcher and clamped between two racks) goes over the drip pan. The top of the box is a large steel tray filled with charcoal so the meat cooks beneath the heat rather than over it. A whole pig cooks in about 4 hours. Visit *lacajachina.com* for more information.

A Big Green Egg stand-alone smoker is mounted into a custom wooden cart with wheels, making it easy to move around the patio.

169

Once you have all the accessories, matching soap dispensers and potted herbs finish the look.

Beyond the essentials, adding a few accessories to an outdoor kitchen will transform it from a place to cook occasionally to a station for preparing entire meals more often. An additional burner opens up a world of possibilities, as you can heat water for pasta, steam some vegetables, boil shellfish, or even make pancakes.

Running water and a sink mean you can clean fruit and vegetables and wash tools, and having a built-in refrigerator means no more trips back and forth to the indoor kitchen during your preparations. The price tag may resemble that of an indoor kitchen remodel, but for some households, the convenience is worth every penny.

BURNERS, SINKS, AND REFRIGERATORS   The stuff that indoor kitchens are made of.

Burners

Burners are available in gas or electric models. If you already have a gas line hooked up to the grill, it's best to tap into that line. For charcoal grills, it may be too costly to run a gas line just for the burner, so an electric model makes more sense. If you haven't bought a grill yet and know you'll want a side burner, look for a combination grill. Some burners have accessories to accommodate woks for stir-fry and griddles for pancakes.

Refrigerators

Powering an outdoor mini-refrigerator may make sense only when the outdoor kitchen gets near-daily action and is a long walk from the indoor kitchen. Be sure to buy a model made specifically for outdoor use. These front-vented models can be installed under the counter, or they can be freestanding if protected from rain by a patio roof.

Sinks and Faucets

Running water makes an outdoor kitchen down-right luxurious, but it requires running a cold-water line and waste line (see pages 100–101). Stainless-steel and enameled cast-iron sinks will stand up to the elements, and you'll likely need only a bar-size model. Buy a high-quality faucet and cover it during the off-season. People who live in areas with freezing winters will need to drain the faucet and pipes before the first frost.

accessories

Check the accessories available from your grill manufacturer. They likely include attachments that allow you to cook everything from breakfast to dessert on your grill.

CHIMNEY STARTERS Facilitate lighting without lighter fluids and speed up the process of readying coals.

SLIDE-OUT TRAY TANKS Gentler on your back when it's time to replace the propane tank.

GRILL COVERS Keep dirt from accumulating on the surface and water from seeping into the cabinets below.

ROAST RACKS Hold up large cuts of meat or potatoes and other vegetables so they are cooked indirectly.

GRILL PAN Use a grill pan instead of aluminum foil when you want small foods like bay shrimp to have that smoky grill flavor.

GRILL LIGHTS Make it possible to cook late into the evening. Some are freestanding, while others attach to the handle or hood of the grill.

GRIDDLES Flat surface makes cooking pancakes and bacon possible.

BRUSH AND SCRAPER Indispensable for cleaning cooking grates.

KEBOB SET Skewers keep kebobs away from direct heat, easy to maneuver.

PIZZA STONE Pizza on the grill? Weber makes it possible with this cordierite ceramic stone that absorbs excess moisture and distributes heat evenly for a crispy crust.

VEGETABLE BASKET When you don't have a side burner, you can still cook vegetables over the grill with this stainless-steel pan.

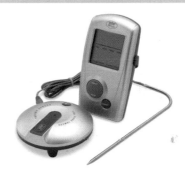

THERMOMETERS Know if your meat is cooked to the right temperature without cutting into it.

GRILL BASKET Holds fragile fish or sandwiches together so they don't fall apart on the grill.

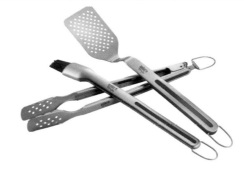

COOKING TOOLS Tools for the grill have longer handles than those for indoor cooking. A spatula, tongs, and a brush are necessities.

RIB RACK Holds ribs and other cuts of meat upright, allowing you to cook more at once.

grilling
basics

Set the table and get ready to wow your guests with the recipes in this section.

We've assembled some of *Sunset's* best grilling recipes to help you make the most of your new outdoor kitchen. But before digging in, read this page for valuable advice from food editors Elaine Johnson and Margo True. Here's on preparing your grill for the recipes in this section.

Gas or Charcoal?

It's your choice. Cooking with gas versus charcoal is a little like driving an automatic versus a stick, and both have their fans. Gas is easy—just turn it on and you're good to go. With charcoal, you have to interact with the fire to keep the food cooking at the right temperature—adjusting the air flow, moving the coals, adding a bit more fuel, and doing a lot of impromptu shifting of the food to whichever spot is at the right heat. Some cooks feel that charcoal gives food a more "grilled" flavor, but gas aficionados tend to disagree.

Direct Heat Grilling

When a recipe calls for direct heat, that means the fire is right beneath the food.

Direct Heat with Gas

Open the lid, press the ignition, turn all burners to high, close the lid, and wait 10 minutes or so for the grill to get hot. Then adjust the burners for the temperature range you need. As you cook, keep the lid closed as much as possible.

Direct Heat with Charcoal

Ignite the charcoal. Our favorite way to start a charcoal fire is with a chimney starter: Stash a few pieces of crumpled newspaper in its base, then fill with charcoal to the top of the chimney starter. Set the chimney on the firegrate (the bottom grate) and open the vents underneath the grill. Ignite the paper and let the fire burn until all the charcoal ignites, 15 to 20 minutes.

» **Spread it out.** Protecting your hands, dump the charcoal onto the firegrate and spread it out with tongs. Then put the cooking grate in place to preheat and let the coals burn to the heat specified in your recipe—usually 5 to 10 minutes for high (see "Taking Your Grill's Temperature," right).
» **Add food.** Arrange your food on the cooking grate; grill with the lid on (and its vents open) for the most even cooking.
» **Adjust the vents.** If you need to reduce the fire's temperature, partially close the vents in the lid and beneath the firegrate. (This will limit the oxygen that feeds the fire.)

Indirect Heat Grilling

In a recipe that calls for indirect heat, the fire burns to one side of the food or all around it rather than directly beneath.

Indirect Heat with Gas

Set a drip pan on one burner, either on the side of the grill or in the middle—it doesn't really matter. With the grill lid open, ignite all the burners and turn them to high. Close the lid and wait 10 minutes or so for the grill to get hot. Turn off the burner with the drip pan on it and adjust the other burners to get the temperature you need. When the grill is at the right heat, set the food over the drip pan. As you cook, keep the lid closed.

Indirect Heat with Charcoal

Ignite the charcoal. Following the steps under "Direct Heat with Charcoal" (left), light the charcoal—using about two-thirds the amount you would need to cover the entire firegrate.

» **Bank it.** When coals are ignited, after 15 to 20 minutes, bank them on opposite sides of the firegrate (bottom grate). Set a drip pan in the empty area and set the cooking grate in place to preheat. Let the coals burn to the heat specified in your recipe, usually 5 to 10 minutes for high (see "Taking Your Grill's Temperature," below).
» **Add food.** The area over the section cleared of coals is the indirect-heat area; set food on the cooking grate above cleared section. Cover the grill, being sure all vents are open.
» **Maintain the heat.** If you're cooking for longer than 30 minutes, add 10 to 12 briquets to the fire every 30 minutes, and leave the fire uncovered for a few minutes to help them light. At the same time, sweep ash from the firegrate by moving the outside lever; this keeps vents clear and air flowing.

taking your grill's temperature

» Some grills have built-in thermometers to guide you, but if not, use the following "hand test." Measure the temperature often. With charcoal, you may have to move food to different spots as it cooks.

VERY HIGH
550° to 650°; you can hold your hand 5 in. above the cooking grate only 1 to 2 seconds.

MEDIUM
350° to 450°; you can hold your hand 5 in. above the cooking grate only 5 to 7 seconds.

HIGH
450° to 550°; you can hold your hand 5 in. above the cooking grate only 2 to 4 seconds.

LOW
250° to 350°; you can hold your hand 5 in. above the cooking grate only 8 to 10 seconds.

**Grilled chicken kebabs
with Romesco sauce**

center (cut to test) and onions are charred in places, about 4 minutes. Serve hot, accom- panied by sauce.

*Smoked Spanish paprika is available at well-stocked grocery and specialty-foods stores.

PER SERVING 533 CAL., 47% (252 CAL.) FROM FAT; 56 G PROTEIN; 28 G FAT (4.2 G SAT.); 14 G CARBO (2.9 G FIBER); 495 MG SODIUM; 132 MG CHOL.

Barbecued chicken

From chef Tyler Florence, everything you could want in a piece of barbecued chicken: moist meat, crisp skin, and tangy sauce.

SERVES 8 | ABOUT 2 HOURS

BRINE AND CHICKEN

2 tbsp. kosher salt

¼ cup packed light brown sugar

2 garlic cloves, smashed

4 sprigs thyme

8 chicken quarters (7 to 8 lbs. total)

BARBECUE SAUCE

1 slice bacon

10 to 12 sprigs thyme

About 2 tbsp. extra-virgin olive oil

½ onion, chopped

2 garlic cloves, chopped

2 cups ketchup

¼ cup packed light brown sugar

¼ cup molasses

2 tbsp. red or white wine vinegar

1 tbsp. dry mustard

1 tsp. *each* ground cumin, paprika, and freshly ground black pepper

1. Make brine: Mix first four ingredients with 2 qts. water in a 2-gal. resealable plastic bag. Add chicken, seal, and chill for 15 minutes to 2 hours.

2. Make sauce: Wrap bacon around thyme; tie with kitchen twine. Heat 2 tbsp. oil in a saucepan over medium heat. Add thyme bundle and cook 3 to 4 minutes. Add onion and garlic. Cook over medium-low heat, stirring until softened, about 5 minutes. Stir in remaining ingredients and cook over low heat, covered, 20 minutes. Remove thyme; spoon half of sauce into a bowl.

3. Prepare a gas barbecue for direct two-level heat (500° to 550°

Grilled chicken kebabs with Romesco sauce

Romesco sauce comes from the Spanish province of Catalonia. You'll need eight 8-in. metal or wooden skewers for grilling.

SERVES 4 | 40 MINUTES

2 lbs. skinned, boned chicken breast halves, cut into 1½-in. cubes

½ cup chopped cilantro

½ cup extra-virgin olive oil, divided

2 tbsp. fresh lime juice

2 tsp. plus 1 tbsp. minced garlic

1 tsp. *each* kosher salt and sweet smoked Spanish paprika*

½ tsp. freshly ground black pepper

¾ cup roasted red peppers

¼ cup whole almonds or hazelnuts, toasted

1 slice crusty bread, toasted and cut into cubes

1 tbsp. sherry vinegar

2 bunches green onions, trimmed

1. If using wooden skewers, soak in cold water at least 30 minutes. In a large bowl or resealable plastic bag, combine chicken, cilantro, 3 tbsp. oil, the lime juice, 2 tsp. garlic, the salt, smoked paprika, and pepper. Toss to coat, then marinate, chilled, 25 minutes.

2. Meanwhile, put roasted peppers, nuts, bread, vinegar, remaining 1 tbsp. garlic, and ¼ cup oil in a food processor and purée; sauce will be thick.

3. Prepare a charcoal or gas grill for direct medium-high heat (about 450°). Thread chicken onto skewers, discarding marinade. Drizzle green onions with remaining 1 tbsp. oil. Lay skewers on cooking grate (close lid on gas grill) and grill 4 minutes. Turn skewers over, then lay green onions on grill. Grill until chicken is browned and no longer pink in

Barbecued chicken

Grilled cilantro chicken with pickled tomato and avocado salsa

in one area and about 300° in another). Wipe cooking grate with oiled paper towels. Pat chicken dry with more paper towels, sprinkle with salt, and drizzle with some oil.

4. Grill chicken skin side down on high-heat area, covered, 5 to 7 minutes. Move pieces to the lower heat, turning over, and cook 20 minutes, covered. Spoon sauce from pan onto skin side and cook chicken until an instant-read thermometer measures 160° at thickest part (or cut to test), 15 to 20 minutes more. Let rest 5 minutes. Serve with sauce in bowl.

PER PIECE 590 CAL., 44% (258 CAL.) FROM FAT; 49 G PROTEIN; 29 G FAT (7.4 G SAT.); 34 G CARBO (1.3 G FIBER); 1,014 MG SODIUM; 155 MG CHOL.

Grilled cilantro chicken with pickled tomato and avocado salsa

We're nuts about this unusual recipe from Mary Sue Milliken and Susan Feniger of Ciudad in Los Angeles and Border Grill in Santa Monica and Las Vegas.

SERVES 4 | 1½ HOURS, PLUS 1 HOUR TO CHILL SALSA

SALSA

1 lb. medium beefsteak-type tomatoes, quartered and seeds squeezed out

2 serrano chiles, stemmed and thinly sliced

½ cup *each* thinly sliced green onions and distilled white vinegar

2½ tbsp. packed brown sugar

1½ tsp. kosher salt

4 tsp. minced fresh ginger

1 tbsp. minced garlic

2 tsp. *each* mustard seeds, freshly cracked pepper, and ground cumin

1 tsp. cayenne

½ tsp. turmeric

½ cup extra-virgin olive oil

2 firm-ripe avocados, pitted, peeled, and cut into ¾-in. chunks

CHICKEN

¼ cup *each* extra-virgin olive oil and fresh lime juice

½ cup chopped cilantro

1 tbsp. ground cumin

½ tsp. *each* kosher salt and freshly ground black pepper

4 skin-on, bone-in chicken breast halves (2½ lbs. total)

1. Make salsa: In a large bowl, combine tomatoes, chiles, and onions. In a medium saucepan over high heat, bring vinegar to a boil. Add brown sugar and salt and cook, stirring, until dissolved, about 1 minute. Remove from heat. Put ginger, garlic, and dry spices in a bowl. In another medium saucepan, heat oil over medium-high heat until rippling. Add ginger mixture and cook, stirring, until fragrant, 1 minute.

Remove from heat, stir in vinegar, and pour over tomato mixtures.

2. Let salsa cool, then cover and chill at least 1 hour and up to 4 hours. About 1 hour before serving, stir avocados into salsa and bring to room temperature.

3. Make chicken: In a large bowl, combine oil, lime juice, cilantro, cumin, salt, and pepper. Turn chicken in mixture to coat. Let stand at room temperature, turning occasionally, for 30 to 45 minutes.

4. Prepare a charcoal or gas grill for direct high heat (450° to 550°). Lift chicken from marinade (discard marinade) and grill (close lid on gas grill), turning often to prevent scorching, until no longer pink at bone (cut to test), 15 to 20 minutes.

5. Transfer chicken to a platter and spoon salsa on top, saving half for another use.

PER SERVING 746 CAL., 64% (477 CAL.) FROM FAT; 50 G PROTEIN; 53 G FAT (9.2 G SAT.); 23 G CARBO (4.9 G FIBER); 591 MG SODIUM; 129 MG CHOL.

Grilled pork chops with onion-peach marmalade

Herb-rubbed baby back ribs with cherry-Zinfandel sauce

Grilled pork chops with onion-peach marmalade

Because modern pork is very lean, the meat can easily dry out. Using a brine adds moisture and flavor.

SERVES 4 | 1 HOUR, PLUS OVERNIGHT TO BRINE

½ cup plus 1 tsp. kosher salt

½ cup packed light brown sugar

1 sprig plus 2 tsp. chopped rosemary leaves

3 tsp. black peppercorns, divided

4 bone-in center-cut pork chops (1¾ lbs. total), fat trimmed

3 tbsp. extra-virgin olive oil, divided

4 cups sliced white onions

2 cups chopped peeled ripe peaches*

⅓ cup granulated sugar

3 tbsp. sherry vinegar

1. Make brine: In a large pot, bring 7 cups water to a boil. Remove from heat and add ½ cup salt, the brown sugar, rosemary sprig, and 2 tsp. peppercorns, stirring until salt and sugar are dissolved. Add 1 cup ice cubes and chill until cold. Immerse pork in brine and set a plate on top of pork to keep it completely submerged. Cover with plastic wrap and chill overnight.

2. Heat 2 tbsp. oil in a large frying pan over medium heat. Add onions and cook, stirring often, until transparent and starting to brown, 10 to 15 minutes. Lower heat to low; add peaches, granulated sugar, vinegar, and remaining 1 tsp. peppercorns. Cook, stirring often, until marmalade is caramelized and sticky, about 40 minutes. Stir in remaining 1 tsp. salt and 2 tsp. rosemary.

3. Prepare a charcoal or gas grill for direct medium heat (350° to 450°). Remove pork from brine and pat dry. Brush chops all over with remaining 1 tbsp. oil. Lay pork on cooking grate. Close lid on grill and cook pork, turning once, until done to your liking, about 10 minutes for medium (an instant-read thermometer inserted into center of thickest part registers 145°). Transfer pork to a platter, tent with foil, and let rest 5 to 10 minutes. Serve with warm marmalade.

*Or use frozen.

Make ahead: Marmalade, 1 day, chilled; reheat to serve.

PER SERVING 526 CAL., 41% (216 CAL.) FROM FAT; 34 G PROTEIN; 24 G FAT (6.5 G SAT.); 44 G CARBO (4.3 G FIBER); SODIUM N/A; 88 MG CHOL.

Herb-rubbed baby back ribs

The pepper in the rub picks up on the black-pepper notes in the Zinfandel sauce.

SERVES 6 TO 8 | 2 HOURS

¼ cup paprika

3 tbsp. dried thyme

1 tbsp. salt, plus more to taste

1½ tbsp. freshly ground black pepper

3 racks pork baby back ribs (7 to 8 lbs. total)

Cherry-Zinfandel Barbecue Sauce (recipe follows)

1. Mix paprika, thyme, salt, and pepper. Pat ribs dry, then rub herb mixture over both sides of each rack, pressing so it sticks. Wrap each rack in heavy-duty foil.

2. Prepare a charcoal or gas grill for indirect medium heat (350° to 450°), using a drip pan filled halfway with warm water.

3. Lay foil-wrapped ribs on grill, meaty (convex) side up, over indirect heat area; overlap slightly if necessary. Close lid on grill and cook ribs until tender when pierced (through foil), 1 to 1¼ hours.

4. Carefully remove foil from ribs. Brush meaty side of each rack lightly with barbecue sauce, turn over, and cook until sauce is browned, about 10 minutes. Brush bone (concave) sides, turn again, and cook until browned on that side, about 10 minutes more.

5. Transfer ribs to a board and cut between bones into individual ribs. Season to taste with salt and serve with remaining barbecue sauce.

Make ahead: Through step 1, up to a day, chilled; bring to room temperature before grilling.

PER SERVING 813 CAL., 69% (558 CAL.) FROM FAT; 51 G PROTEIN; 62 G FAT (23 G SAT.); 11 G CARBO (0.6 G FIBER); 1,229 MG SODIUM; 242 MG CHOL.

Cherry-Zinfandel barbecue sauce

This sauce is packed with the flavors of Zinfandel—dried cherries, anise seeds (Zin often has faint licorice flavors), black pepper—and lots of the wine itself.

MAKES 3½ CUPS | 40 MINUTES

1 tbsp. extra-virgin olive oil
1 medium onion, chopped
2 tbsp. chopped garlic
1½ cups dry red Zinfandel wine
1 cup ketchup
⅔ cup dried tart cherries
3 tbsp. cider vinegar
3 tbsp. Worcestershire
3 tbsp. packed light brown
    sugar
2 tbsp. Dijon mustard
2 tbsp. chopped fresh ginger
1 tsp. anise seeds
1 tsp. freshly ground black pepper
¼ tsp. cayenne
2 tbsp. fresh lemon juice,
    plus more to taste

1. Heat oil in a medium saucepan over medium-high heat until hot. Add onion and garlic and cook, stirring often, until limp, 3 to 4 minutes. Add remaining ingredients except lemon juice. Bring to a boil, then reduce heat and simmer, stirring occasionally, until liquid begins to thicken slightly, about 20 minutes. Let cool slightly.

2. Pour mixture into a blender, add lemon juice, and purée. Taste and add more lemon juice if you like. Use warm or at room temperature.

Make ahead: Up to 3 days, chilled; bring to room temperature before using.

PER ¼ CUP 70 CAL., 14% (10 CAL.) FROM FAT; 0.8 G PROTEIN; 1.1 G FAT (0.1 G SAT.); 15 G CARBO (0.5 G FIBER); 294 MG SODIUM; 0 MG CHOL.

Char siu–glazed pork and pineapple buns

Chinese-style barbecued pork, or char siu, *is popular throughout the Hawaiian Islands. We like to serve these tangy-sweet, meaty little buns at a cocktail-party version of the luau.*

SERVES 12 | 1 HOUR, PLUS
3 HOURS TO BRINE

¼ cup kosher salt
¼ cup packed light brown sugar
1 tbsp. Hawaiian vanilla extract*
2 pork tenderloins (about 1 lb. each)
½ cup ketchup
½ cup hoisin sauce
2 tbsp. toasted sesame oil
2 tbsp. minced garlic
2 tbsp. minced fresh ginger
2 tbsp. reduced-sodium soy sauce
12 slices peeled, cored fresh
    pineapple
24 King's Hawaiian sweet rolls or
    other small soft rolls, warmed
    on the grill if you like
1 cup cilantro sprigs

1. Make brine: In a large pot, bring 3½ cups water to a boil. Stir in salt, brown sugar, and vanilla. Chill until cool.

2. Put pork in a 9- by 13-in. pan and pour on brine. Chill at least 3 hours and up to 12.

Char siu–glazed pork and pineapple buns

3. Make char siu glaze: In a small bowl, mix together ketchup, hoisin, sesame oil, garlic, ginger, and soy sauce. Pour half of sauce into another small bowl.

4. Prepare a charcoal or gas grill for indirect medium heat (350° to 450°). Remove pork from brine. Lay pork over indirect heat area, close lid on grill, and cook until an instant-read thermometer inserted into thickest part registers 135°, 15 to 20 minutes.

5. Using a pastry brush and one bowl of glaze, cover pork with glaze, reserving 2 tbsp. for pineapple. Cook pork (if you're using charcoal, add 6 to 8 briquets to maintain temperature), turning occasionally, until glaze has caramelized slightly and meat registers 145°, 5 to 10 minutes. Transfer grilled pork to a cutting board, tent with foil, and let rest 15 minutes.

6. Lay pineapple on direct heat area of grill, brush with reserved glaze, and cook, turning once, until grill marks appear. Remove slices from grill and cut in half.

7. Cut pork into ½-in.-thick slices. Cut a deep diagonal slit across top of each roll, then fill with a piece of pork, a grilled pineapple slice, a cilantro sprig, and ½ tsp. glaze from second bowl. Serve rolls with remaining glaze.

Buy at gourmet grocery stores and hawaiianvanilla.com; non-Hawaiian vanilla extract works too.

Make ahead: Brine pork and make char siu glaze up to 1 day ahead and chill.

PER SERVING 424 CAL., 25% (108 CAL.) FROM FAT; 26 G PROTEIN; 12 G FAT (5.2 G SAT.); 53 G CARBO (3.2 G FIBER); 823 MG SODIUM; 87 MG CHOL.

Grilled king salmon with asparagus, morels, and leeks

5. Set salmon on foil on cooking grate; grill, covered, until fish is barely cooked through, about 10 minutes. With 2 wide spatulas, slide fish from skin to a warm platter; tent with foil. If you want crisp skin, continue to cook skin on foil until crisp, 1 to 3 minutes more. Remove foil from grill, then gently peel off skin, using fingers or a wide spatula (skin may break into pieces).

6. Add cream and asparagus to mushrooms and bring to a boil over high heat, stirring; boil longer to thicken sauce if you like. Set salmon skin, if using, on a platter. With 2 spatulas, set fish on skin. Spoon half the vegetable sauce over salmon and serve the rest on the side. Serve immediately.

Soak dried morels in hot water until softened, 8 minutes. Squeeze out water; cut in half.

PER SERVING 448 CAL., 71% (316 CAL.) FROM FAT; 25 G PROTEIN; 35 G FAT (15 G SAT.); 8.7 G CARBO (2.7 G FIBER); 366 MG SODIUM; 132 MG CHOL.

Baja light fish tacos

A good fish taco, a cold Corona, and the beach equal summer up and down the coast of California—on both sides of the border.

MAKES 12 TO 14 TACOS | 1 HOUR

1 tbsp. ancho chile powder
2 tsp. dried Mexican oregano
¼ tsp. kosher salt
¼ tsp. pepper
1½ lbs. boned, skinned Pacific cod
1 tbsp. olive oil
12 to 14 corn tortillas (5 to 6 in.), warmed on grill
Cabbage and Cilantro Slaw and Light Chipotle Tartar Sauce (recipes follow)

1. Prepare a charcoal or gas grill for direct high heat (450° to 550°). Combine seasonings in a small bowl. Set fish on a rimmed baking sheet. Rub all over with oil, then sprinkle with seasonings. Oil cooking grate, using tongs and a wad of oiled paper towels.

2. Grill fish, covered, turning once, until just cooked through, 4 to

Grilled king salmon with asparagus, and leeks

This splurge-worthy recipe comes from chef Kevin Davis of Steelhead Diner and Blueacre Seafood in Seattle.

SERVES 6 | 1¼ HOURS

1 lb. slender asparagus, trimmed and cut in half on a diagonal
1 large leek (white part only), thinly sliced and rinsed well
3 tbsp. butter
2 tsp. chopped fresh thyme leaves
¾ tsp. kosher salt, divided
½ tsp. pepper, divided
½ lb. fresh morel mushrooms, rinsed well and halved lengthwise, or ¾ oz. dried morels*
¼ cup fino sherry or dry white wine
1 tbsp. extra-virgin olive oil
1 king or coho salmon fillet (1½ lbs., 1 in. thick), with skin
1 cup whipping cream

1. Boil asparagus until barely tender-crisp, 2 minutes; drain and rinse asparagus in cold water.

2. Prepare a charcoal or gas grill for direct medium-high heat (about 450°).

3. In a large frying pan over medium heat, sauté leek in butter until soft, 5 minutes. Add thyme, ½ tsp. salt, ¼ tsp. pepper, and the morels; cook, stirring occasionally, until morels are tender, 5 minutes. Stir in sherry and reduce by half, 30 to 45 seconds. Set aside.

4. Fold a 12- by 17-in. sheet of heavy-duty foil in half crosswise. With a knife tip, poke dime-size holes through foil 2 in. apart. Oil one side of foil. Rub fish on both sides with oil and put skin side down on oiled foil. Sprinkle with remaining ¼ tsp. *each* salt and pepper.

Baja light
fish tacos

**Grass-fed burgers with
chipotle barbecue sauce**

6 minutes total. Break fish into large chunks. Fill tortillas with slaw and fish. Serve with tartar sauce.

Cabbage and cilantro slaw
Put 3 tbsp. fresh lime juice, 2 tbsp. vegetable oil, ¼ tsp. red chile flakes, and ½ tsp. kosher salt in a large bowl. Just before serving, toss with 1 bag (10 oz.) very finely shredded cabbage and ⅓ cup chopped fresh cilantro.

Light chipotle tartar sauce
Seed and devein 2 tbsp. canned chipotle chiles; rinse. In a blender, purée chiles, 8 oz. (1 cup) plain low-fat Greek yogurt, ¼ cup sweet pickle relish, and ¼ cup chopped onion.

PER TACO WITH 1 TBSP. SAUCE 151 CAL., 27% (41 CAL.) FROM FAT; 10 G PROTEIN; 4.7 G FAT (0.6 G SAT.); 18 G CARBO (1.9 G FIBER); 210 MG SODIUM; 17 MG CHOL.

Grass-fed burgers with chipotle barbecue sauce
You'll have plenty of the spicy, tangy sauce left over—try it with grilled chicken or ribs.

SERVES 4 | 35 MINUTES

CHIPOTLE BARBECUE SAUCE
¼ cup packed light brown sugar
½ cup ketchup
2 tbsp. canned chipotle chiles in adobo sauce (about 3 chiles), plus 1 tbsp. sauce
1 tbsp. Worcestershire
2 tbsp. molasses
2 tbsp. thawed orange juice concentrate
1 tsp. minced garlic
BURGERS
1¼ lbs. grass-fed ground beef
2 tsp. kosher salt, divided
2 tsp. freshly ground black pepper, divided
1 red onion, cut ¼ to ½ in. thick crosswise

3 tsp. vegetable oil, divided
4 slices Swiss cheese
4 sesame-seed hamburger buns
4 slices ripe tomato
4 butter or romaine lettuce leaves

1. Make chipotle barbecue sauce: Purée all sauce ingredients in a blender or food processor until very smooth.

2. Make burgers: In a medium bowl, combine beef and 1½ tsp. *each* salt and pepper. Form into 4 patties, each about ¾ in. thick and slightly thinner in the center (burgers will even out while cooking). Put on a plate, cover, and chill until ready to grill.

3. Prepare a charcoal or gas grill for direct medium heat (350° to 450°).

4. Sprinkle onion slices with remaining ½ tsp. *each* salt and pepper and 1 tsp. oil. Grill, covered, until softened, turning once,

about 8 minutes total.

5. Meanwhile, rub burgers with remaining 2 tsp. oil and lay on grill. Close lid on grill and cook burgers, turning once, about 6 minutes total for medium-rare. In last few moments of cooking, lay a slice of cheese on each burger. Lay bun halves, cut side down, on cooking grate to toast slightly.

6. Transfer buns to a platter and add burgers and onions to bun bottoms. Spoon about 1½ tbsp. barbecue sauce on top of each and add a slice of tomato, a lettuce leaf, and bun tops.

Make ahead: Sauce, 1 week, chilled.

PER BURGER, WITH 1½ TBSP. SAUCE AND TRIMMINGS 612 CAL., 50% (306 CAL.) FROM FAT; 36 G PROTEIN; 34 G FAT (14 G SAT.); 41 G CARBO (2.3 G FIBER); 1,175 MG SODIUM; 112 MG CHOL.

**Grilled grass-fed rib-eyes
with herb lemon butter**

1. Blend ingredients in a food processor until smooth, about 2 minutes.
2. Lay a piece of plastic wrap on a work surface. Using a rubber spatula, scrape butter lengthwise onto plastic. Lift top edge of plastic up and over butter to meet bottom edge of plastic. Roll butter toward you, forming a log about 4 in. long. Twist ends of plastic to close. Chill until firm, about 30 minutes.
3. Remove plastic and slice off ¼-in. portions (1 tbsp.) to serve over steaks.

Make ahead: Up to 1 week chilled, or up to 1 month frozen, wrapped in several layers of plastic.

PER TBSP. 54 CAL., 96% (52 CAL.) FROM FAT; 0.2 G PROTEIN; 5.8 G FAT (3.6 G SAT.); 0.6 G CARBO (0.2 G FIBER); 1.7 MG SODIUM; 16 MG CHOL.

Crazed mom's easy steak and garam masala naan-wiches

Question: Is it possible to make dinner in about an hour while simultaneously grocery shopping for the week? Yes, if you throw a flank steak (very thin, fast-cooking) in a marinade, get someone else in your family to light the fire and set the table, rush off to a nearby grocery store and careen through aisles while piling food in the cart, zoom back home, and toss the meat on the grill. While steak is cooking, make sauce from the marinade, warm up the bread, and put watercress in a bowl. Slice the meat and sit down to eat!

SERVES 6 | 20 MINUTES, PLUS 1 HOUR TO MARINATE

¼ cup extra-virgin olive oil
1½ tbsp. fresh lemon juice
1½ tsp. garam masala*
½ tsp. salt, plus more to taste
½ tsp. freshly ground black pepper
1 beef flank steak (about 1 lb.), fat trimmed
6 naan breads, about 3½ by 8 in. (1½ lbs. total)
3 cups very loosely packed watercress sprigs

Grilled grass-fed rib-eyes with herb lemon butter

Nothing shows off the natural, clean flavor of grass-fed beef like a thick, juicy steak.

SERVES 4 | ABOUT 15 MINUTES

4 grass-fed bone-in rib-eye steaks (1 lb. each and about 1 in. thick)
Kosher salt and freshly ground black pepper
Vegetable oil
Herb Lemon Butter (recipe follows)

1. Prepare a charcoal or gas grill for direct medium heat (350° to 450°).
2. Sprinkle each steak generously with salt and pepper; rub with oil. Grill steaks, covered, turning once, until done the way you like, 10 to 12 minutes for medium-rare.
3. Transfer steaks to a large platter and top each with a slice of herb lemon butter.

PER SERVING WITHOUT BUTTER 383 CAL., 47% (180 CAL.) FROM FAT; 48 G PROTEIN; 20 G FAT (8 G SAT.); 0 G CARBO; 117 MG SODIUM; 136 MG CHOL.

Herb lemon butter

Compound butter (butter blended with flavorings) is a great and simple way to add taste and texture to beef, chicken, fish, or vegetables.

MAKES 1 CUP | 20 MINUTES, PLUS 30 MINUTES TO CHILL

½ cup unsalted butter, softened
¼ cup *each* chopped fresh basil, cilantro, flat-leaf parsley, mint, and oregano leaves
2 tbsp. fresh lemon juice
Finely shredded zest of 1 lemon
¼ tsp. kosher salt
¼ tsp. freshly ground black pepper

Crazed mom's easy steak and garam masala naan-wiches

Grilled skirt steak (arracheras)

1. In an 8- or 9-in.-square baking dish, mix oil, lemon juice, garam masala, salt, and pepper. Turn steak in mixture and marinate at room temperature 1 hour.

2. Prepare a charcoal or gas grill for direct very high heat (550° to 650°). Pre-heat cooking grate for at least 10 minutes.

3. Pour marinade into a small pan and bring to a simmer; remove from heat. Pour 1 tbsp. water into a blender, turn on, drizzle in marinade, and blend to emulsify.

4. Lay steak on cooking grate, close lid on grill, and grill steak, turning once, about 5 minutes for medium-rare (cut to test). Transfer to a board and loosely cover with foil.

5. Grill naan, turning once, until hot and slightly crusty, 1 to 2 minutes. Transfer to board.

6. Thinly slice steak across grain. Let each person arrange meat and watercress over half of each naan.

Drizzle sauce on top, sprinkle with salt to taste, and fold naan in half to make a sandwich.

Garam masala is available in the spice section of many supermarkets; if you cannot find it, substitute 1 tsp. cinnamon, ½ tsp. each ground cumin and freshly ground black pepper, and ¼ tsp. each ground cardamom, nutmeg, cloves, and cayenne.

PER NAAN-WICH 457 CAL., 41% (189 CAL.) FROM FAT; 25 G PROTEIN; 21 G FAT (6.9 G SAT.); 28 G CARBO (2.9 G FIBER); 764 MG SODIUM; 38 MG CHOL.

Grilled skirt steak (arracheras)

Mexican arracheras, like Tex-Mex fajitas, are marinated skirt steaks cooked quickly over high heat to produce a nicely browned crust and pink interior. This recipe is from Santa Fe barbecue experts Bill Jamison and Cheryl Alters Jamison.

SERVES 6 TO 8 | 40 MINUTES, PLUS 5 HOURS TO MARINATE

2 beef skirt steaks (1 to 1¼ lbs. each), fat and membrane trimmed
1 bottle or can (12 oz.) beer
¼ cup fresh orange juice
¼ cup fresh lime juice
2 to 3 tbsp. chipotle hot sauce, such as Tabasco Chipotle Pepper Sauce, plus more for serving
2 tbsp. minced garlic
1½ tbsp. kosher salt
1½ tsp. ground cumin
3 large red onions, cut into ½-in.-thick slices
Vegetable-oil cooking spray
12 flour tortillas (8 in. wide), warmed
Lime wedges

1. Cut each steak in half crosswise and put in a large resealable plastic bag. Stir together beer, orange juice, lime juice, hot sauce, and garlic, then pour over steaks. Seal bag and refrigerate at least 5 hours and up to overnight.

2. Prepare a charcoal or gas grill for direct medium-high heat (about 450°). Drain meat and discard marinade. Blot dry with paper towels. Mix together salt and cumin and rub into meat.

3. Spray onions lightly with oil and set, with steaks, on cooking grate. Close lid on grill. For medium-rare to medium doneness (cut to test), grill steaks 3 to 4 minutes per side if less than ½ in. thick; add 1 more minute per side if more than ½ in. thick. Turn steaks at least once while grilling. Grill onions, covered, turning once, until browned on both sides and cooked through, 8 to 10 minutes total.

4. Transfer steaks to a platter and let rest 5 minutes. With a sharp knife at a slight diagonal, cut across grain into thin strips. Serve meat and onions with tortillas, lime wedges, and hot sauce.

PER SERVING 463 CAL., 33% (153 CAL.) FROM FAT; 32 G PROTEIN; 17 G FAT (5.1 G SAT.); 43 G CARBO (3.4 G FIBER); 1,345 MG SODIUM; 58 MG CHOL.

Pizza bianca

Coppa, ricotta, arugula pizza

Pizza margherita

Grilled pizza

This dough produces a crisp crust every time. Try the recipe at your next backyard party—the pizzas can be partially grilled ahead of time, then finished in a few minutes.

MAKES 6 INDIVIDUAL PIZZAS
1 HOUR, PLUS 2 HOURS TO RISE

1 package (2¼ tsp.) active dry yeast
6 tbsp. extra-virgin olive oil, divided
4 cups flour
1½ tsp. salt
Your choice of toppings (recipes follow)

1. In the bowl of a stand mixer, stir yeast into 1½ cups warm water (100° to 110°). Let stand until yeast dissolves, about 5 minutes. Add ¼ cup oil, the flour, and salt. Mix with dough hook on low speed to blend, then mix on medium speed until dough is very smooth and stretchy, 8 to 10 minutes. Dough will feel tacky.

2. Cover dough; let rise at room temperature until doubled in bulk, about 1½ hours.

3. Punch down dough and let rise again until doubled, 30 to 45 minutes. Meanwhile, cut six pieces of parchment paper, each about 12 in. long. Prepare a charcoal or gas grill for direct medium heat (350° to 450°).

4. Turn dough out onto a work surface and cut into six portions. For each pizza, lay a sheet of parchment on work surface and rub with 1 tsp. oil. Using well-oiled hands, put each portion of dough on a parchment sheet. Flatten dough portions, then pat into 9- to 10-in. rounds. If dough starts to shrink, let rest 5 minutes, then pat out again. Let pizza dough stand until puffy, about 15 minutes.

5. Flip a round of dough onto cooking grate, dough side down. Peel off parchment. Put on one or two more dough rounds. Close lid and cook until dough has puffed and grill marks appear underneath, 3 minutes. Transfer rounds, grilled side up, to baking sheets. Repeat with remaining dough. (Grilled rounds can stand at room temperature up to 2 hours; reheat grill to continue.)

6. Arrange pizza toppings on grilled side of dough. With a wide spatula, return pizzas, two or three at a time, to cooking grate and close lid on grill. Cook until browned and crisp underneath, rotating pizzas once for even cooking, 4 to 6 minutes.

Make ahead: Complete dough through step 1, then chill, covered, at least 3 hours and up to 2 days (dough will double in size, and flavor will develop as it chills).

Coppa*, ricotta, arugula pizza

Evenly spread 2 heaping spoonfuls (⅓ cup) ricotta cheese onto each half-grilled dough round in step 5 of Grilled Pizza, then top each pizza with 3 slices of coppa. Grill as directed. In a bowl, combine about 2 tbsp. extra-virgin olive oil, a squeeze of fresh lemon juice, and a pinch *each* of salt and freshly ground black pepper; toss with 5 cups (2½ oz.) arugula. About 1 minute before pizzas are done, scatter a generous amount of dressed arugula onto them; close lid on grill and finish grilling, about 1 minute.
**Coppa, sometimes called* capicola, *is a delicious Italian-style cured meat eaten very thinly sliced. You can also use prosciutto, bresaola, or thinly sliced salami.*

PER PIZZA 643 CAL., 45% (288 CAL.) FROM FAT; 22 G PROTEIN; 32 G FAT (9.7 G SAT.); 67 G CARBO (2.8 G FIBER); 980 MG SODIUM; 49 MG CHOL.

Pizza bianca

Scatter a few slices of white onion and a large handful of shredded mozzarella cheese over each half-grilled dough round in step 5 of Grilled Pizza, then sprinkle with chopped fresh rosemary leaves and a little salt. Grill as directed.

PER PIZZA 587 CAL., 41% (243 CAL.) FROM FAT; 20 G PROTEIN; 27 G FAT (9.4 G SAT.); 66 G CARBO (2.6 G FIBER); 796 MG SODIUM; 44 MG CHOL.

Pizza margherita

Spread each half-grilled dough round in step 5 of Grilled Pizza with about 2 tbsp. Ripe Tomato Pizza Sauce (recipe follows). Evenly space 5 or 6 slices drained water-packed fresh mozzarella cheese over sauce. Grill as directed, then top with small whole or torn basil leaves.

PER PIZZA 725 CAL., 45% (324 CAL.) FROM FAT; 27 G PROTEIN; 36 G FAT (14 G SAT.); 73 G CARBO (4.7 G FIBER); 1,001 MG SODIUM; 67 MG CHOL.

Ripe tomato pizza sauce

Heat 1 tbsp. extra-virgin olive oil in a saucepan over medium heat. Add 1 tbsp. minced garlic and cook, stirring, until fragrant, about 1 minute. Stir in 4 large chopped tomatoes, 1 tsp. sugar, ¼ tsp. red chile flakes, and ½ tsp. *each* kosher salt and freshly ground black pepper. Bring to a boil, reduce heat to low, and simmer, stirring often, until very thick, about 1½ hours. Stir in 1 tbsp. chopped fresh oregano leaves. Makes 1 cup.

PER 2-TBSP. SERVING 44 CAL., 43% (19 CAL.) FROM FAT; 1.1 G PROTEIN; 2.1 G FAT (0.3 G SAT.); 6.4 G CARBO (1.5 G FIBER); 83 MG SODIUM; 0 MG CHOL.

Chili-lime corn on the cob

Cooking corn on the cob in its de-silked husk keeps the kernels moist and adds a nice grassy flavor. You can also fully husk the corn and wrap it in foil. This recipe is from California restaurateur and Food Network personality Guy Fieri.

SERVES 6 | 35 MINUTES

Chili-lime corn on the cob

Japanese tofu skewers on soba

¼ cup butter, softened

1 tsp. finely shredded lime zest

1 tsp. chili powder

½ tsp. salt, plus more for serving

½ tsp. freshly ground black pepper

¼ tsp. granulated garlic

6 ears unhusked corn

1. Combine butter, lime zest, chili powder, salt, pepper, and garlic in a small resealable plastic bag. Mush around to combine thoroughly.

2. Pull back husk from each ear without detaching from bottom of cob. Remove as much silk as possible. Spread ears evenly with butter mixture. Fold husks back over ears and tie in place with kitchen string or strips torn from outer husks.

3. Prepare a charcoal or gas grill for indirect medium heat (350° to 450°). Set corn over indirect heat area and close lid on grill; cook corn until tender and charred,

about 20 minutes. Serve with salt for sprinkling.

Make ahead: Through step 2 up to 24 hours, chilled.

PER SERVING 112 CAL., 39% (44 CAL.) FROM FAT; 3 G PROTEIN; 4.9 G FAT (2.5 G SAT.); 17 G CARBO (2.5 G FIBER); 150 MG SODIUM; 10 MG CHOL.

Japanese tofu skewers on soba

Tofu holds up beautifully on the grill as long as you use the firm nigari kind. You'll need four 10- to 12-in. metal or wooden skewers.

SERVES 2 TO 4 | 40 MINUTES

½ cup reduced-sodium soy sauce

½ cup mirin (sweet rice wine)

2 tbsp. toasted sesame oil

10 to 12 oz. nigari tofu*, cut into 1-in. cubes

16 small fresh shiitake mushroom caps

2 tbsp. vegetable oil

4 green onions, cut into 1½-in. lengths

12 oz. dried soba noodles

8 radishes, thinly sliced

⅔ cup reduced-sodium vegetable broth

2 tsp. wasabi paste

1 tsp. finely shredded lemon zest

¼ cup fresh lemon juice

1. If using wooden skewers, soak in cold water at least 30 minutes. Prepare a charcoal or gas grill for direct medium heat (350° to 450°).

2. Mix soy sauce, mirin, and sesame oil in a bowl. Add tofu and marinate 10 minutes.

3. Heat a large pot of water to boiling. In a bowl, toss mushrooms in oil to coat.

4. Drain tofu, reserving marinade. Slip cubes onto skewers, alternating with green onions and mushrooms. Thinly slice any leftover onion.

5. Boil noodles in water until al dente, 4 minutes. Drain; rinse well

with cold water. Divide noodles among dinner bowls and garnish with radishes and sliced onion.

6. Oil cooking grate, using tongs and a wad of oiled paper towels. Grill tofu skewers, covered, turning once, until lightly browned, 6 to 8 minutes. Set skewers on noodles.

7. Mix marinade with broth, wasabi, lemon zest, and juice and serve on the side.

Buy nigari in the refrigerated section of your grocery store.

PER SKEWER PLUS ¼ OF NOODLES 595 CAL., 28% (169 CAL.) FROM FAT; 23 G PROTEIN; 19 G FAT (2.3 G SAT.); 85 G CARBO (2.2 G FIBER); 1,900 MG SODIUM; 0 MG CHOL.

resources

Vase by Maison Reve; pitcher and glasses by Crate and Barrel.

The following organizations, manufacturers, and retailers are mentioned or have products shown in this book. They can help to outfit your new outdoor kitchen and dining area.

Associations and Organizations

National Fire Protection Association
www.nfpa.org

American Society of Landscape Architects
www.asla.org

Association of Professional Landscape Designers
www.apld.com

Building Materials Reuse Association
www.buildingreuse.org

Forest Stewardship Council
www.fsc.org
Nonprofit organization established to promote the responsible management of the world's forests

Grills, Pizza Ovens, and Appliances

Barbeques Galore
www.bbqgalore.com

Big Green Egg
www.biggreenegg.com
Smokers

Char-Broil
www.charbroil.com

Dacor
www.dacor.com

Ducane
www.ducane.com

Fiesta Grills
www.fiestagasgrills.com

Fogazzo Wood Fired Ovens and BBQs
www.fogazzo.com

The Home Depot
www.homedepot.com

Jenn-Air
www.jennair.com

Kenmore Grills
www.kenmore.com

La Caja China
www.lacajachina.com
Roasting boxes

Lowe's Home Improvement
www.lowes.com

Lynx Professional Grills
www.lynxgrills.com

Marvel Refrigerators
www.marvelscientific.com

Mugnaini
www.mugnaini.com

Napoleon Grills
www.napoleongrills.com

Vermont Castings
www.vermontcastings.com

Viking
www.vikingrange.com

Weber
www.weber.com

Accessories

Blue Rhino
www.bluerhino.com
Propane, outdoor heaters

Crate and Barrel
www.crateandbarrel.com

Danver
www.danver.com
Stainless-steel cabinetry

Erica Tanov
www.ericatanov.com
Linens

Gaiam
www.gaiam.com
Eco-friendly outdoor furniture and accessories

Hable Construction
www.hableconstruction.com
Home and garden products

IKEA
www.ikea.com

Koolfog
www.koolfog.com
Outdoor misters

Maison Reve
www.maisonreve.com
Home and garden products

The Pampered Chef
www.pamperedchef.com
Grilling accessories and outdoor dishes

Pottery Barn
www.potterybarn.com

Rev-A-Shelf
www.rev-a-shelf.com
Cabinet pullouts and accessories

Shade Sails
www.shadesails.com
Tensioned fabric canopies

Smith & Hawken
www.smithandhawken.com
Outdoor rugs, furniture, and accessories

Sunbrella
www.sunbrella.com
Outdoor fabric

Sur la Table
www.surlatable.com

Tom's Outdoor Furniture
www.tomsoutdoorfurniture.com

Williams-Sonoma
www.williams-sonoma.com

Finish Materials

Buddy Rhodes
www.buddyrhodes.com
Concrete countertop mix and sealants

Eldorado Stone
www.eldoradostone.com
Faux stone and prefabricated counters

Heath Ceramics
www.heathceramics.com
Handmade tile

Trex Co.
www.trex.com
Composite decking

photography credits

© William Abranowicz Art + Commerce: 22; Jean Allsop and Harry Taylor: 163 right (architecture: Folck West + Savage; interior design: Lovelace Interiors); Iain Bagwell: 180 (food styling: Randy Mon); Leigh Beisch: 177 left (food styling: Dan Becker; prop styling: Sara Slavin), 178 left (food styling: Dan Becker), 178 right (food styling: Karen Shinto; prop styling: Emma Starr Jensen), 182 left (food styling: Dan Becker; prop styling: Sara Slavin); Annabelle Breakey: 185 left (food styling: Karen Shinto), 185 right (food styling: Karen Shinto; prop styling: Emma Starr Jensen), 177 right (food styling: Karen Shinto), 179 left (food styling: Karen Shinto; prop styling: Emma Starr Jensen), 179 right (food styling: Dan Becker), 181 left (food styling: Randy Mon), 181 right (food styling: Dan Becker), 182 right (food styling: Karen Shinto; prop styling: Emma Starr Jensen); Nicola Browne/GAP Photos: 149 left (design: Steve Martino), 26 (design: Topher Delaney); Wayne Cable: 96 top row left, 96 middle row center, 96 bottom row left, 96 bottom row right, 97 row 1 center, 97 row 3 center, 97 row 5 right; courtesy of Cal Flame: 167 bottom; Jennifer Cheung: 102 (pizza oven: Woodstone), 130, 136, 138, 33

(design: Jason Isenberg); Torie Chugg/The Garden Collection: 23; courtesy of Robinson Brick: 147 top center left; Daley + Gross: 110; Sergio de Paula: 99 top, 100 left; Laura Dunkin-Hubby: 96 bottom row center; Liz Eddison/The Garden Collection: 126, 171 center; Eldorado Stone and Reimers & Hollar Photographers: 118, 119 all; Fhfgreenmedia/GAP Photos: 32 top right; courtesy of Fire Magic: 168 top center, 173 top left; Scott Fitzgerrell: 147 bottom right; Roger Foley: 159 bottom right (design: James David); Frank Gaglione: 97 row 2 right, 111 all, 112 all, 113 all; 123 all, 147 top left, 147 bottom center left, 148 left (landscape architects: Ransohoff, Blanchfield, Jones Inc.), 149 right, 171 right, 173 bottom left; Tria Giovan: 15 both, 24; Leo Gong: 176 (food styling: Dan Becker); Thayer Allison Gowdy: 183 (food styling: Dan Becker; prop styling: Emma Starr Jensen); Art Gray: 156; Jack Halloway: 151 center left; Jerry Harpur/Harpur Garden Images: 27 top (design: Topher Delaney); Margot Hartford: 162 right, 163 left; Tom Haynes: 147 top right, 147 bottom left; Maree Homer/acp syndication.com/JBG Photo: 154; IPC+ Syndication: 157 top left; Simon Kenny/acpsyndication.com/JBG Photo: 116; Chuck Kuhn: 151 center right; Geoff Lung/f8 Photo Library: 7 both, 29 top right, 157 bottom; courtesy of Lynx Grills: 172 top center; Red Cover/Peter Margonelli: 18; Andre Martin/acpsyndication.com/JBG Photo: 98, 165; Ericka McConnell: 30; Red Cover/Anastassios Mentis: 8; Minh+Wass: 158; Minh+Wass/StockFood: 159 bottom left; MMGI/Marianne Majerus: 114 (design: Charlotte Rowe), 170 (design: Declan Buckley); Gary Moss/FoodPix/Getty Images: 166; Laura Moss: 28; Mike Newling: front cover (Kate Stickley, Arterra Landscape Architects; Kevin Brush, contractor; Elements Landscape; styling:

Philippine Scali and Jack Halloway), 1 (David Jochum, Polsky Perlstein Architects; Michael B. Yandle Landscape Architecture; Bob Klock Builder; styling: Philippine Scali and Jack Halloway; plates and tray from Pottery Barn), 9 top (styling: Philippine Scali and Jack Halloway), 42–43 (Karen Taylor, Polsky Perlstein Architects; Caitlin Landscape Architecture; Power Construction, general contractor; styling: Philippine Scali and Jack Halloway), 44–45 (Keith Willig Landscape Architecture and Construction; styling: Philippine Scali and Jack Halloway; chairs by Tom's Outdoor Furniture; vase from Maison Reve; pitcher and glasses from Crate and Barrel), 46 left (styling: Philippine Scali and Jack Halloway), 46 right (styling: Philippine Scali and Jack Halloway), 48 (Karen Taylor, Polsky Perlstein Architects; Caitlin Landscape Architecture; Power Construction, general contractor; styling: Philippine Scali and Jack Halloway), 49 (styling: Philippine Scali and Jack Halloway), 51 (styling: Philippine Scali and Jack Halloway), 52–53 (Keith Willig Landscape Architecture and Construction; Rosemary Wells, Viridian Landscape Architecture; styling: Philippine Scali and Jack Halloway), 55 both (styling: Philippine Scali and Jack Halloway), 56–57 (Kate Stickley, Arterra Landscape Architects; Elements Landscape; styling: Philippine Scali and Jack Halloway), 59 (styling: Philippine Scali and Jack Halloway), 60 both (styling: Philippine Scali and Jack Halloway), 61 (styling: Philippine Scali and Jack Halloway), 62 (Keith Willig Landscape Architecture and Construction; styling: Philippine Scali and Jack Halloway), 63 (styling: Philippine Scali and Jack Halloway), 65 (styling: Philippine Scali and Jack Halloway), 66–67 (James Dibble, landscape contractor; Michael B. Yandle Landscape Architecture; Dan Zazzeron Masonry; styling: Philippine Scali and Jack Halloway), 68 both (styling: Philippine Scali and

Jack Halloway; drink container from Pottery Barn; tray from Sur la Table), 70–71 (Kate Stickley, Arterra Landscape Architects; Siteworks, landscape contractor; styling: Philippine Scali and Jack Halloway; galvanized accessories from Pottery Barn,), 73 both (styling: Philippine Scali and Jack Halloway), 74–75 (Mara Young, landscape architect; Charles Smith, Gentry Landscapes; Geri Martin Wilson; styling: Philippine Scali and Jack Halloway; bar stools from Sundance, www.sundancecatalog.com; plates and galvanized accessories from Pottery Barn; salad bowl by Heath Ceramics), 76 both (styling: Philippine Scali and Jack Halloway), 78–79 (Kate Stickley, Arterra Landscape Architects; Kevin Brush, contractor; Elements Landscape; styling: Philippine Scali and Jack Halloway; lanterns and laquered tray from West Elm, www.westelm.com; rug and umbrella from Pottery Barn), 82 left (styling: Philippine Scali and Jack Halloway; lanterns and laquered tray from West Elm, www.westelm.com; rug and umbrella from Pottery Barn), 82 right (styling: Philippine Scali and Jack Halloway), 83 (styling: Philippine Scali and Jack Halloway), 84–85 (Don Modica, Modica Landscaping; Hernandez Welding; styling: Philippine Scali and Jack Halloway), 87 both (styling: Philippine Scali and Jack Halloway), 88–89 (Keith Willig Landscape Architecture and Construction; styling: Philippine Scali and Jack Halloway; runner from Maison Reve), 90 (styling: Philippine Scali and Jack Halloway), 92–93 (Vera Gates, Arterra Landscape Architects, Arcanum, architect; Plemons Construction; styling: Philippine Scali and Jack Halloway; barstools from Tom's Outdoor Furniture; wicker tray from Pottery Barn), 94 both (styling: Philippine Scali and Jack Halloway), 186 (styling: Philippine Scali and Jack Halloway; chairs by Tom's Outdoor Furniture; vase from Maison Reve; pitcher and glasses from Crate and Barrel, 188

(Keith Willig Landscape Architecture and Construction; styling: Philippine Scali and Jack Halloway; runner from Maison Reve), 190 (Kate Stickley, Arterra Landscape Architects; Elements Landscape; styling: Philippine Scali and Jack Halloway), 120 (styling: Philippine Scali and Jack Halloway), 142 (styling: Philippine Scali and Jack Halloway), back cover all (styling: Philippine Scali and Jack Halloway); **Philipp Newton:** 9 bottom; **Clive Nichols/Photolibrary:** 11; **Red Cover/Anthony Parkinson:** 25; **Norm Plate:** 31 bottom (Jim Pollack Design); **Norman A. Plate:** 35 (design: Peter O. Whiteley); **Red Cover/Practical Pictures:** 10, 151 right (design: Alan Gray Graham Robeson); **Kylie Rae/acpsyndication.com/JBG Photo:** 27 bottom; **Paul Raeside/Livingetc/IPC+ Syndication:** 162 left; **Lisa Romerein:** 12, 13 both, 16, 20, 21, 31 top, 40 bottom, 41 (styling: Valerie Aikman Smith); **Lisa Romerein/Getty Images:** 174; **Mark Roper/acpsyndication.com/JBG Photo:** 32 top left; **Eric Roth:** 4–5, 29 top left, 37, 106, 116; **Mark Rutherford:** 101 all, 96 top row right, 96 middle row right, 97 row 4 center; **Loren Santow:** 103 top left, 103 top right, 103 bottom left, 103 bottom right; **David Schiff:** 96 middle row left, 97 row 1 left, 97 row 1 right, 97 row 2 left, 97 row 2 center, 97 row 3 left, 97 row 3 right, 97 row 4 left, 97 row 4 right, 97 row 5 left, 97 row 5 center; **Mark Scott/Woman & Home/IPC+ Syndication:** 29 bottom; **Thomas J. Story:** 6, 40 top left (Perry Becker, Perlman Architects, Scottsdale, AZ), 145 (landscape design: Antonia Bava Architects), 152, 153 bottom right,

155 bottom right (Stefan Thuilot with Joseph Huettl, Huettl Thuliot Associates), 160, 184 (food styling: Randy Mon); **Tim Street-Porter:** 34, 36, 38 bottom, 153 top right, 157 top right, 159 top left, 159 top right, 161 bottom left, 164, 169; **Dan Stultz:** 115 all, 121 bottom left, 121 bottom center, 121 bottom right, 131 all, 132 all, 133 all, 147 bottom center right; **Dave Toht:** 100 right, 103 bottom center, 104, 105 all, 107 all, 108 all, 109 all, 117 all, 121 top #1, 121 top #2, 121 top #3, 121 top right, 125 all, 127 all, 128 all, 129 all, 137 all, 140 all, 141 all, 143 all; **Nicola Stocken Tomkins/The Garden Collection:** 19; **E. Spencer Toy:** 146, 168 bottom; **Red Cover/Debi Trelor:** 157 top center; **Mark Turner:** 122; **Mikkel Vang/Taverne Agency:** 161 bottom right; **Dominique Vorillon:** 14, 38 top; **Julian Wass:** 40 top right; **courtesy of Weber:** 167 top, 168 top left, 168 top right, 172 top left, 172 top right, 172 bottom left, 172 bottom center, 172 bottom right, 173 top center, 173 top right, 173 middle left, 173 middle center, 173 middle right, 173 bottom center, 173 bottom right; **Michael Wee/acp syndication.com/JBG Photo:** 150, 153 bottom left; **Lee Anne White:** 151 left (Clemens & Associates, Inc.), 155 top (Desert Sage Builders); **Lee Anne White/Photolibrary:** 17; **Red Cover/Mark Williams:** 39; **Michele Lee Willson:** 148 right (Brian Koch, Terra Ferma Landscapes), 153 top left (Ken Coverdell-Blue Sky Designs, Inc.); **Brent Wilson/acpsyndication.com/JBG Photo:** 155 bottom left, 171 left; **Polly Wreford/Homes & Gardens/IPC+ Syndication:** 32 bottom, 161 top

Special Thanks

Mark Hawkins, Elaine Johnson, Laura Martin, Brianne McElhiney, Kimberley Navabpour, Marie Pence, Linda Lamb Peters, Alan Phinney, Lorraine Reno, Vanessa Speckman, E. Spencer Toy. Thank you to the homeowners who graciously allowed us to photograph their outdoor kitchens and the designers and builders who shared their work.

index